Observations of an Orchestrated Catastrophe

curious theatre branch • contemporary theater collection

Observations of an Orchestrated Catastrophe

plays and performances

Jenny Magnus

Observations of an Orchestrated Catastrophe

plays and performances

Jenny Magnus

For more information on this book or to order, visit
www.jacklegpress.org

Published by
JackLeg Press
Washington, DC

ReIssue w/ new Foreword © 2021 Jenny Magnus
ISBN-13: 978-1-7373307-2-1

First Publication Printing © 2014 Jenny Magnus
ISBN-13: 978-1494445003 / ISBN-10: 149444500X

All rights reserved
Printed in the United States of America

No part of this work may be reproduced or utilized in any form or by any means, electronic or mechanical, including photocopying, microfilm, digital scan and recording, or by any information storage and retrieval system, without permission in writing from the publisher.

Library of Congress Cataloging-in-Publication Data

Book Design by Jason Greenberg / Art Works Design

Photo Credits:
Front/Back Cover & Artist Profile images by Jeffrey Bivens
Frontispiece image by Joe Mazza / Brave Lux
The Willies by Tamara Staples
The Trips and *The Lucky Ones* by Curious Theatre Branch
The Strange and *Round & Round* by Christopher Dimock
How To Carry Love and *Nowhere But Up* by Jeffrey Bivens
Room by Jenny Magnus
Still In Play by Kristin Basta

ACKNOWLEDGEMENTS

This book is dedicated to:
Stefan Brün, Bryn Magnus, and Beau O'Reilly,
my permanent readers, for all my long life; and
to you, Audience, how I love/hate you…

The work in this book was produced by, with,
and for The Curious Theatre Branch.

Thanks to:
Lena Luna Magnus Brün, for whom everything…;
Jennifer Harris and Jackleg Press;
Julie Williams, my tender amanuensis;
The Magnus Family; The Brun Family;
Jeffrey Bivens; all my wonderful Curious comrades;
all those who trudge with me; and of course,
a special thanks to BO'R, for his collection…

General Notes on the Text:

Songs in-text are indicated with bold titles and *(sung)*.
All the musics in this book can be found on my website,
jennymagnus.com and **curioustheatrebranch.com**.

The songs that have been released on albums
were supported and hosted by 8th Day Records
and Uvulittle Records.

Titles of individual pieces within pieces are not necessarily
to be spoken, but they could be.

Unless otherwise indicated, roles can be played by
performers of any gender or age. I did it the way I did it,
but you should do these the way you would do them.

Observations of an Orch

estrated Catastrophe:

TABLE OF CONTENTS

Sections / Plays

Re-Introduction; Author's Foreword — 12

Preface: The Original Introduction — 16

The Willies: A Performance of Incubus and Succubus — 20

The Trips: A Madras Parable — 46

The Lucky Ones — 79

The Strange — 110

Round and Round: a sexfarcetragedy — 140

How To Carry Love: A Play with Futon and Bag of Rice — 220

Room — 246

Nowhere But Up — 260

Still In Play: A Performance of Getting Ready — 276

Outroduction — 320

Artist Profile — 322

FOREWORD

A RE-INTRODUCTION

Nothing Into Something

by Jenny Magnus

March, 2021

I never remember writing anything. It is all conjured, out of thin air, from nothing to something, in a fugue state of will. Everything has to be right: the room, the air, the sounds, the mood, the derangement, the hopelessness. If anything is not right, nothing comes out of the nothing, and nothing is made into something. For these reasons it is very difficult for me to write at home. At home, I am a person who mothers, who takes care of others, a tiddle toddle domestic mama sort of person, attending and scheduling and guiding and guilting. My at home derangement is about others, and whether I have held them up or held them down. My writing life derangement is about myself- my own mental banquetry of unmaking and aspiration, of dank unformed thoughts and plasticity of personality. I despair in writing, I find it difficult to despair out loud at home. There are other people to think of, they don't want to see that. So I secret myself away to write, I take myself away, as far away as I can get, from who I am, from who is needing me, and that means I can fall into that fugue and be in the cloud of unknowing. To-do lists are not salient there.

I am seeing this collection of writing all as if new, not remembering it. I am reading it, thinking, why is this idea stated this way? Why does this make sense? What is she trying to say? The great benefit of writing amnesia is that I am able to read for meaning, instead of reading for flaws or self-criticism. I am reading to understand what that person, who wrote that thing, at that time, is trying to communicate to me, the reader. So as I read the work I wrote, over 20 years, from 1990-2010, I am discovering what that lady, that struggling lady of the tiddle toddle body, has been trying to say.

First there is the theme of attention. It really struck me, when I read these works over, how much I had been thinking about how to pay attention, whether I was in fact paying attention, and in particular, in *Cruise Control* from *The Willies*, whether one could ever possibly pay attention to all the things that need it. From *The Willies* to *Still in Play*, the characters have a dawning awareness that they may have missed something terribly important when they were busily attending to something else.

Another common thread I found was a strong urge towards connection, whether it be with another person or with the self, and how difficult and twistedy those connecting communications can be. In *The Trips*, the characters Sop and Heave use their goofings around and games to try and co-exist in the hidey hole of their partnership, reading each other and calling each other out, but always together in their interminable journey. When Beau O'Reilly and I first performed this work, in the 90's at the old Links Hall, we hadn't entirely memorized the script, and we had papers on our music stands, which represented the car/steering wheel. At one point, one of us knocked into the music stand inadvertently, and the papers went flying. The reviewer thought it was brilliant, the metaphor of scrambling through the pages to find where the hell we were in the script.

The games people play also figure in prominently thoughout. In *Round and Round*, the games are explicit, a bunch of preposterous disguises and wagers and secrets. It was very important to me that the moustache was super obviously fake, and yet, was believed by the people who have bought into the game. In some of the work, the games are formal, like the recurring dialogue fragment word play in *The Lucky Ones*, based around the words "I don't want this." The formal game of how to use a futon as an arena, where all the terms are worked out between lovers, that then transforms into a bag of rice the weight of a child, which is the consequence of the futon, in *How to Carry Love*. The formal game of portraying the hour before the play begins, in *Still in Play*, which actually takes around 75 minutes, but hey, time spent together in preparation is liminal and sometimes interminable. Also, the actual playing of ductball, a Curious Theatre Branch staple, figures prominently. You can't perform ductball, you can only play ductball.

This world is teetery, more so than ever before in my lifetime, and that shifting dizziness is hard to navigate. I think the only way out is through, not to coin a phrase, and we all have to be willing to climb up on the piles of shit and junk of the world, and start picking out the stuff that is reclaimable, salvageable, and start building something new. Even if the new thing is a fraught, painful, weird, frightening thing, we can start again. Because we don't lose everything we have learned up to the point of collapse- we bring all that with us into the next thing. Even if we forget for a moment, we can look back and read what we wrote, and think to ourselves, ok, that IS something out of nothing.

If I could do it that time, I can do it again.

PREFACE

AN INTRODUCTION

"Ask me something hard. Ask me something tricky. Ask me something secret. Ask me something dangerous. Ask me something interesting. Ask me something ambiguous." This is the invitation—a kind of dare, really—that Jenny Magnus proffers in *The Trips*, probably one of her best known and most admired scripts. Note the imperative: there's something not so much commanding as compelling in the phrasing. It is a prompt not to interrogate but to collaborate. In this way, the artist and the audience will investigate together.

Then look again: Ask me something hard. Let's make it challenging.

And again: Ask me something secret, something dangerous.
Let's chance exposure, chance vulnerability.

Ask me something ambiguous—let's be brave enough
to complicate the question.

In these plays, Magnus is asking us to meet her intelligence, her wit, the naked soul of her unknowables with our own because, in her work, the question is the quest.

Like Brecht, she uses music, text, broad characters, very few props. Her people are curious and smart and very funny. They are always out on a limb, divulging something terribly embarrassing. They use a lot of words, or very few. Metaphors are often over-the-top, but particulars can be few. The fourth wall, when it's there, is just a flimsy film—which means the performers who take on these stories must be experienced high-flyers, actors who know the consequences of working without a net.

In Magnus' stories, characters have unexplained encounters that are so lively and absurd that it takes a moment to realize they are in pain. The pain is sometimes mysterious in origin, sometimes as sharp as a spear point, often uncomfortable to listen to. But it is also a deeply, deeply honest pain: stripped down, fearless in its emotional complexity, uncompromising in its directness and contradictions.

"Sometimes we fuck things up beyond repair," Magnus says in *The Strange*.

In other words, what to do—how do we go on with our lives—when there's no mending the rupture or erasing the scar? Sure, we can learn to live with the consequences—but not by surrendering to them, not by "accepting" them except to grapple mano a mano with them forever. There's just no rest for the lazy in these scripts.

Here is the work of an artist as courageous as you'll ever experience.
Here is the work of an artist timeless and true.
Relish it.

– Achy Obejas, 2013

THE PLAYS

1994 – 2011

Jenny Magnus in *The Willies*

The Willies: A Performance of Incubus and Succubus

Premiered 1994
Organic Greenhouse
Chicago, IL

performed by Jenny Magnus

The Willies: A Performance of Incubus and Succubus

SETTING

The stage is set with a vertical bed and a chair, the merest sketch of a bedroom. The bed is a piece of plywood, standing almost straight up and down, but on a slight incline. A sheet, blanket, and pillow are attached to the "bed," so that it looks like the performer is lying in the bed when she is leaning against it...

The lighting suggests the middle of the night. Lights fade up on the performer, in the bed, tossing and turning. For each monologue, the performer will assume the persona of a character, get out of the bed, inhabit the "room," and speak...

One: Smelling

(Sniffing around) I smell something…Do you smell that? I'm smelling something…You don't smell that? Wow, I can really smell something. I don't like smells. I consider them very gross. There are a lot of smells where I live, but I didn't think there would be any here. My house really smells. I cleaned. Thoroughly. But I could still smell something. It's been getting worse. I got a headache just waking up the other day. So I came here. But now I smell something here. When is the last time you cleaned? I don't mean to be rude, but I am really smelling something. It's hard to describe, it's kind of like a…it's kind of like a bad smell.

(Realizing) Maybe it's me. I smell it here and there. What could it be? I wash. Often. I washed before I came here. *(Smells everywhere)* I can't tell. Listen, come here. Let me ask you…do I smell? Let me smell you. I don't think it's you. Maybe it is me. I am really smelling it. This is very…This is exactly why I came here. Because I just couldn't take it anymore. And now here it is as well. This is so…

(Realizing) Maybe it's not…on me. Maybe it's in me. Maybe something inside of me smells bad. That would explain why no one else can smell it. Because I'm smelling it from inside. I've never heard of that, have you? Do you think it's going to get worse? What could it be? What have I eaten? I haven't eaten anything bad. I haven't felt sick, just sickened by the smell. Maybe I'm thinking about it all wrong. Maybe it isn't something I've eaten at all, and maybe I'm not sick, maybe it's something…

rotten inside of me. Maybe I am rotting and I can smell it. Why would I be rotting? Do people just spontaneously rot? Or do they have to do something first? Or not do something? I wonder if I've done anything to start myself rotting? I haven't been neglectful or filthy. I've been very moderate in my habits. In fact everything about me has been very moderate, except for how I feel about this smell. I intensely dislike it. I have always been very moderate.

But since this smell has been bothering me, I have been more irritable. I do feel upset more. Because I just haven't been able to escape it. The more I think of it the more I feel like the end of my being moderate coincides exactly with the beginning of this smell. It's very very bad. I can see now that it has to do with my moderation being over. I'm not sure yet whether I think that my moderation has given over to being worse or better, but it does seem to have gone. And since it's gone I have become aware of the constant presence of this smell, which, as I say, is very bad. So as I think about it, it seems that I must have <u>gone</u> bad, as opposed to good, because if I had turned from moderate to good, wouldn't I smell something good?

Yes, I'm convinced of it now, I'm smelling the rot of my own badness. I still don't know if I'm rotting because I am bad, or if I am bad because I am rotten, but in a way it doesn't matter. I do feel relieved now that I have figured it out. And as long as no one else can smell it, maybe it won't be so bad, maybe I can actually get used to it. You know people can get used to anything.

> (Goes back to bed, lights indicate a shift...Another person is now in the bed, a different kind of agitation. They also cannot sleep. This person is more finicky, a lady, prim in a Tennessee Williams-ish way, clutching at her bedclothes. She gets up, goes and sits in the chair.)

Two: A Swift Kick

I don't think of myself as being difficult. It's just that I get ahold of something and it's real hard to shake it loose. It's like a farmdog on a mailman's pants leg, I know I'm going too far with it, and I expect a swift kick, but I just have to work it. Usually, I'm real aware of how people are seeing me, but this time I must have plain missed it, because I surely did not expect the outcome. Here is what happened, you can judge it for yourself…

My desk is right next to the desk of Miss Angela Kitterling. She and I are not the best of friends, but we had always operated under a system of mutual respect and co-existence. Contrary to what some folks believe, I do not hold her responsible for the events that caused my downfall, though there might be some good reason to suspect that she was enjoying them as they occurred. Knowing Miss Angela Kitterling the way that I do, I have learned that the left side of her mouth moves in a peculiar way when she is greedily sucking up gossip or lying, so she is as close to an open book to me as is my copy of the *Book of Lists* that I have in my bathroom. See, she can't fool me. This is part of the problem between us, is that I can see virtually right through her. Miss Angela Kitterling is not clever, she is merely cunning, and many people mistake that for being naïve. They can't imagine that she would be the way that she is and not have some shred of self-dignity or whatever… I am just certain, that if others could see Miss Angela Kitterling through my eyes, things would be very different. Very different.

Anyway, as I have said, Miss Angela Kitterling's desk and mine adjoin one another, and for a good long while, we had an unspoken agreement to share the view of a vase and flowers.

One or the other of us would make sure that there was some seasonal sprig in that vase to help us through the long days. I myself have always been partial to a lovely flower, while Miss Angela Kitterling's taste has tended to run towards the non-flowering twig-like varieties of arrangements, of which I find no fault, I simply prefer the other. One day, it just so happened that I was feeling blue. I arrived with what I must assume was an air of melancholy, so much so that Miss Angela Kitterling commented upon it. I am, like many terribly sensitive people, subject to great oceans of distress and morbidity in my thinking, and I am capable of torturing myself mercilessly until I rise above it again, and am more able to shoulder the burdens of my existence.

On this particular day, I must have been very much inside myself, because by the time I had looked up, Miss Angela Kitterling was gone. And then, sooner than you could say snap, crackle, and pop, she was walking in with the most beautiful bouquet of flowers one could possibly imagine. And, they just happened to be pink gladioli, which are my all time favorite bloom. Well, it must have shown upon my face, my pleasure and surprise, because the next day, and the next, and the next after that, and so on for many days, Miss Angela Kitterling not only made me the gift of so many lovely bouquets, she also placed the vase upon my desk and mine alone, so that I could have the superior view of it. I am a trusting soul. It never once occurred to me to question the actions of Miss Angela Kitterling. In fact, after a point, I felt that I would reciprocate her gesture, and I even said, "Miss Angela Kitterling, wouldn't you prefer a pussy willow, or a mimosa branch, or a cattail or two?" Now mind, we had never discussed any of this before. Perhaps this is where I am at fault, speaking the unspoken, but I felt that it behooved me to try and understand just where she was coming from. These events were unprecedented and perhaps I was thrown a little off balance by them.

Well, Miss Angela Kitterling assured me in the most affable and pleasant way that she was deeply enjoying my pleasure, and it would only please her all the more to see me pleased…or something like that. So I put it out of my mind. This was my terrible mistake. I allowed Miss Angela Kitterling to insinuate herself into my life and my heart, without so much as a by-your-leave. Before I knew it, we were friends. *(Emphatically)* And so much more. I found myself deeply and desperately in love with Miss Angela Kitterling and she with me. *(Emphatically again)* Or so I thought. Because, as it turned out, Miss Angela Kitterling was spending her every-other-Sunday-afternoon, which was a time we had agreed not to meet, with someone else. And not just anyone else, mind you, but with a <u>man</u>. With a Mr. Joshua Fanter.

I still, after all this time, become incensed when I speak of it. Can you imagine the gall? Can you!? I have spent many a sleepless night imagining it, believe you me. For Miss Angela Kitterling to have betrayed me, with Mr. Joshua Fanter, why I could wring his scrawny neck like a Christmas goose. All of our kisses, all lies. It is a chapter that is now closed forever. I was drawn in by her smile and I simply grabbed hold and would not let go. Until it was too late, and Miss Angela Kitterling was forced to hurt me and destroy me. And do you know what she said? She told me that there was nothing going on. That I had made the entire thing up. That for some reason I did not want to live in our love, and that she was certain I would have found any excuse, and, now she said this, that if I could even think about her and Mr. Joshua Fanter together that I was mentally imbalanced. I have never in my life been so shocked. That she would so baldly lie to me…

I feel as if I have been the victim of some bloody war. There is no comfort for me in the arms of another. I have observed Miss Angela Kitterling flinging herself at one person and the next, with no regard for their qualities, simply to humiliate me and remind me that she is very well off without me indeed. If only I had never allowed myself to believe that there was goodness in the world, I would be contented to live out my days quietly. But no, I had to get ahold of Miss Angela Kitterling and not want to let go. I have always been waiting for that swift kick, for as long as I can remember. It is my nature.

> *(She makes her teary, irate way back to the bed...*
> *Lights shift, another character emerges...A person with such agitation, it propels them out of the bed. They have something to say, but it will not emerge without some building of pressure...It builds and builds, and then, explosion. This person is unhinged. The monologue is delivered in as few breaths as possible, running each breath through the ends of long sentences.)*

Three: Eureka!

Dear Gene Hackman!...I am telling this to you because last night I saw your movie Eureka! and I just had to tell you that the exact same thing happened to me that happened to you in the movie...You know how when you were searching for the gold for those 15 years in the Yukon and you seemed like you would be crazy and just die alone out there frozen under the tree like your partner that you left there to die because you were so obsessed with finding the gold that you couldn't stop?...And then you fell into the mother load completely by accident and it was so incredible that you shot out of the hole on a geyser of gold and you had that moment where everything you were searching for your whole life actually was <u>found</u> and you were in the cavern of gold where it was so beautiful and it meant you were going to be so rich that you would never ever have to even think about money again…and how from then on your entire life was like an afterthought because the most important incredible amazing moment of your life had already happened and nothing else could ever live up to it again, not the wildest sex or the most beautiful love or the most terrifying anything?...Well, that is why I am telling this to you, Gene Hackman, because the same thing happened to me and I didn't even know that it had until I saw your movie last night. Only I didn't find gold or anything like that, it was a different kind of thing but I felt the way you felt in that movie. What happened to me was that I saw something. I saw something that no living person is supposed to see and keep on living because it kind of blew my mind, Gene! It kind of changed me in this way that's hard to understand except now I can see it as a *Eureka!* kind of thing…

I was standing on the corner of the main street in Madison, Wisconsin at 3:00 on October 8, 2008 and I was looking at all the people walking around going about their business, and all of a sudden I saw that everyone I could see, everyone on the street and the busses and on the bikes and in the shops, everyone was dead! They were all dead! And I looked around at all of them and I was in shock because they had all seemed normal one instant ago and then I remember my mind saying now you're going to get really scared because everyone is dead and then the really amazing thing happened, I didn't get scared, Gene, I felt so happy! I felt like something so beautiful was happening to me, like a miracle because I realized or actually it was not a dawning kind of thing like a realization, but a knowing, like I had known it all along and had forgotten it until that exact moment, I understood that everyone who was ever born, everyone who was alive, who had <u>ever</u> lived, was going to die or was already dead, that everyone died! And then I thought, and I am going to die. I looked at my hand and I saw it was dead, that it was going to die eventually, inevitably, I would be dead, and Gene, Gene, it was such a relief! Because it was like everything evened out in this weird flat plane and I could see my life, the whole thing, all stretching out away from me in these strings touching each of the people around me and all the people I knew and I could see their strings reaching out and touching me and all the people around them, and I could see all their lives and deaths like weird flat stories but visible and alive, like living stories, and it was like they were all so beautiful and interesting, and I felt like what was important was not things that happened or didn't happen in life, but life was important, these weird flat strings were important, death was important…Oh Gene, it was so weird and amazing and I wasn't doing drugs or anything like that Gene, it was a totally spontaneous experience…It was so weird Gene, and I haven't even described it right but I just stood there looking at all the dead people and I felt like it was so funny and amazing that I had ever cared for one second about my rent or anything like that because I was going to die and that was the only thing that was real.

I stood there for a long time and it gradually turned back into a normal seeming day and yet I was totally different, I couldn't do anything I had ever done before and my life has taken this turn, I haven't been able to keep ahold of that feeling and for a long time I have felt so lost and cheated in a weird way, like, why have I kept being alive if the only thing that is real is being dead?

(Long pause.)

Gene, the only way I can think of to describe it is…it's like, thinking you're farting, but really, you're shitting…

(Character returns to bed, or could be a blackout, and lights up to reveal the next character in bed. This is clearly a man, 30 something, as physically male as it is possible to convey, the kind of guy who takes up all the room on the train, legs sprawled. He is confident but with a dawning doubt of himself…He is giving up on sleep, not visibly agitated, already in the surrender of knowing that sleep is not coming. He gets up, goes and sits down…)

Four: Cruise Control

My philosophy is don't regret anything. Much to my surprise that works pretty well. Surprise? Well, sometimes things happen that seem, uh, regrettable, but I'm not talking about fault, I'm talking about that other feeling, that you just wish things could have gone another way. Of course you can't change anything once it's done, but now and then you have a lingering sense that you could have done better. Or differently.

But hey, don't get the idea that I'm an uptight kind of person, worrying or tense. I'm loose, I like to let things flow. You know, I've got this car with cruise control. This is the greatest invention since sliced bread. You get behind the wheel, get out of the city, and kick back. It really changes the whole dynamic of driving. It's like being taken, you fly along. It's very freeing. It changes the whole calculation, other cars seem to float alongside, you're all part of a solid river, no stress, just movement. It's hypnotizing, you can't think of yourself as the driver of the car. It drives itself, you just steer.

I, uh…I've been going through kind of a hard time. I'm out of it now, I'm on the other side of it, and I can look back on it more objectively. I realize that the damage you do to yourself, it's worse than any person could do to you. I just think that being in the now, being in the present, that's your best bet. Otherwise, the odds are all against you, especially the older you get. When you're young, no matter what happens to you, no matter what you do, there's always time to do something else. I mean, there's plenty of time to, you know, be an asshole. You can always redeem yourself later. When you're young, you're un-selfconscious, there are so many firsts, all the time. But then you lose your innocence. It can't last. You do things, you do them again. You do them again and again.

I mean, like the first time you fuck...You're starting from zip, so everything's forgivable. You're greedy, you want to come, you want to taste it, you can't wait. But that just can't last. I mean, like the first time you get somebody pregnant, that's a lesson. You do the right thing, you take her to the place, you pay for the abortion, whatever, you act sweet, you're not glad that it happened, you wonder why she didn't use birth control. The first time, it's forgivable. But hey, the next couple of times, if you don't start to learn from it, you're just being... Oh, what's that word...It's on the tip of my tongue...Willful. That's it, it's like you don't <u>want</u> to learn. But like I said, no regrets. You just have to figure out how to analyze your experiences and not repeat them. Because you can't stay un-selfconscious forever. Sooner or later you're going to find out that the way you might naturally be or what you might do left to your own devices may not be acceptable to other people.

I've got this friend. He's an art teacher. He told me about a class of really little kids he was teaching, like 4-5 year olds, and they would sit on stools pulled up around a big table, and he would teach them how to papier maché and stuff. Well, there was this one girl in the class, the youngest one, maybe only 3 years old, but one day she was really squirming around and he asked her, did she have to go to the bathroom? She said, nah, but all day she kept squirming around. Then he realized that she was, like, jerking off, right there, on the stool, totally un-selfconscious. Just giving herself a lot of pleasure. My friend didn't know what to do. It didn't seem to be particularly bothersome to any of the other kids, but he kept watching her, he couldn't help himself. It wasn't like he was getting off on it, it was more like fascinating to him. He said he couldn't help but wonder when that kid was going to be told to stop doing that, and how she would take it.

Even now as an adult, I'm going along, not thinking, and I'll realize with a kind of start that I'm scratching myself. I'll be talking to someone and I'll find my hand down my pants, playing around with my balls or something. And it's embarrassing, to wake up to that fact that you don't even know you're doing it.

That's my biggest hurdle. To stay present but not regret anything. There are some things I set aside. They're different. It's like a class of things. I've been thinking a lot about something that happened to me…That's funny, in a way it didn't happen to me as much as it happened to someone else. But I did it. To them. Sort of. A few months ago I was driving, I was zooming along, I wasn't really thinking about driving, I was cruising, and I…hit a kid. It wasn't my fault, the goddamned kid ran right out, it was chasing, I mean "she" was chasing a ball, I could see it about to happen, but the calculation was different, my foot was nowhere near the brake. I just wasn't paying attention in quite the right way. It didn't make sense to me, that she would run out into the road like that, I mean, didn't anyone teach her about looking both ways? That's what you have to do, teach children what is acceptable behavior. I've never been one of these "let them burn it on the stove to teach them about hot" kind of people. But hey, it was spontaneous on her part, I could see that, even though it happened so fast, she wasn't thinking about the consequences.

I was exonerated. I wasn't held responsible. Not legally. But she's dead. And her parents...her friends...and me...well, we're all changed. I'm more self-conscious than I was before. I feel different.

I was talking to a woman the other night. I really wanted to fuck her. She was sitting next to me, telling me about why I shouldn't want to, she's fucked up, she's confused. But we did it anyway. *(Indignant)*   Then later, she writes me this letter, it's like an indictment. How I took advantage of her. But hey, she's an adult, it wasn't rape or anything close to that, and to be fair, she didn't try to call it that. She just said she was disappointed in me. That I hadn't been <u>kind</u> to her… It made me feel a little scared to think that maybe there's a whole class of things that I'm unaware of. That I am un-selfconscious of. And that I'm going to be forced to pay attention to. I can't quite see how I'm going to stay in the present if there are all of these things I have to pay attention to. It all goes by so fast, it's confusing, and I feel like I'm not really in control of it. Like it's sweeping me along and I only have time to pick up on a few things.

I am working on not regretting anything. It's pretty hard though, I mean, those are only words.

> *(Lights shift, performer goes back to the bed,
> lights up to reveal someone very agitated,
> leaps out of bed, is pacing around and muttering…
> His "ahhh" sounds are like an uncontrollable rictus,
> bursting out of him to one side.)*

Five: Mental Illness

Ahhhh…I can't sleep…I'm frozen, that's it, I've got to admit it to myself…I'm supposed to go in there and make something happen. I can't do it, it's impossible. It's mental illness, that's what it is, mental illness. I mean, they just sit there staring, they think it's easy, they expect it, they expect me to make something happen, but it's not that easy. I mean, I can tell them what to do or what to think, but they won't do it, it's mental illness. I mean, I get an idea, I've got an idea, but so what? It's just an idea, I mean, there's a huge difference between an idea and something that moves around, that has a life. I mean, ahhh my god, I saw a thing, once, where it was all built around the word, "tender." I mean, how brilliant! "Tender." I've never thought about that word the same way since. I mean, my god, how can I do anything after that? It's too hard, I'm frozen…I can't, I can't…

I've got to calm down, this is mental illness, I've done this so many times, I can do it again, I just have to calm down. Ok, I know what to do…It's the elements, think about the elements…Ok, I know this, I know this…Ideas! That's number one, that's first, ideas. I mean, good ideas, good ones. Although dumb ideas are better than no ideas. But ok, that's first, sure, ahhh, ahhh, ahhh…Flesh! That's right, fleshing it out is next. Sitting down and giving it a voice. A character. Right. It's got to have a place to come from, a way of speaking. It's no damn good as a lecture, it's got to be in context. Ok, what next? Then what? A gimmick! A ta-wist, it's got to have a ta-wist, sure, keep it interesting. Nobody just wants a story anymore, got to punch it up, punch it hard…

This is working! This is working…I can do this. *(Like the wicked witch)* I'm melting, that's good. Ok, first: an idea…let's see…got it! A bunch of people, and they're in a room, a big room, and they're talking...No that's shit, come on, ok, forget the room, forget the people...How about this: a rat. Sure, there's a rat, and a...a robot, and they're in hell, together...oh fuck that is terrible, I can't make that work. No no, how about there's these vampires, and they'll suck the life out of people, people who are already vapid! Yes, and they'll be tricking them with some kind of beverage...Oh my god, this is mental illness! Why didn't I just stay in public TV? I give up, it's over, I give up, I will go in there tomorrow and humble myself, I have nothing, nothing...

(Slaps head, is struck. This is it!) Humility! That's an idea. A humble man. Nothing to say. Flesh it, flesh it...an inarticulate, humble silent man, empty, frozen, alone, in a room, at night, can't sleep, tortured, pacing...THIS IS GENIUS! THIS IS GENIUS! And no lines to learn! See, you think it's gone forever, and then, *(snaps fingers)* there it is.

(Lights shift. The performer is in the bed, lying still. The monologue is delivered from the bed, never moving.)

Six: Thinking About Fucking

I can't sleep. I can't stop thinking about fucking. Fucking is fun. When I'm a man, I like to fuck from behind, not harsh but sweet, like a nice dog. When I'm a woman, I like to lie back flat with perfectly spread legs, yielding completely, like the tendons have been neatly cut. Once, I changed half-way through. That poor guy. He was just scared to death. I didn't mean to scare him, it just happened. I got carried away. I was yielding and floating and looking at his flesh, the bruised banana colors, and suddenly I

<u>became</u> the painter-eye objectifier, which is so male in me, and I couldn't just lie there receiving his attentions, I had to embody the urge to formally organize.

It's a good thing I figured out how to change. It happened to me a few times before I learned to control it. I was a woman to begin with and, like a lot of people, it didn't sit quite right with me. A part of me felt invaded by fucking, like having someone put something inside of you was a little presumptuous and insulting. When some guy would put his tongue in my mouth, I would occasionally feel a wave of black atavistic hatred come over me and I would get a murderous impulse to strangle the life out of him by stuffing my fist so far into his mouth that I could feel the muscles of his throat contracting on my forearm…or in my ear…*(shudder)* I like it in the cunt. My clit is a little dingleberry. But it wasn't until I changed into a man for the first time that I really understood the fascination and the impulse to get in there. Anywhere. In. I'm talking about the ride. You know. Or putting the head of my dick in, just the head, in and out like popping a cork in a bottle.

You're uncomfortable aren't you? I'm talking about fucking and it makes you uncomfortable. Is it the words? Do the words make you uncomfortable? Or…maybe you're not uncomfortable. No, it's the changing…You're trying to imagine it. I can do it for you right now, if you want…*(Performer lies still throughout and nothing changes or moves. A long pause.)* You can't see it, can you? You can't tell at all…I was afraid this was going to happen.

(The performer sadly gets out of bed, changes affect to be an effete, tidy man…He stands on the stage, and every so often, jerkily moves his foot, as if to prevent it from becoming stuck.)

Seven: Robert

This is a very unlikely situation. I realize that it strains the credulity of the normal mind, and it certainly is not something I could have ever predicted. For a long time, I simply could not comprehend it. I would say to myself, "Robert, this is not really happening. You've obviously mistaken something explicable for something inexplicable and soon this temporary derangement will cease and you will be your own man again...." And every morning I would wake up thinking things would be back to normal and then they wouldn't be. So recently, I've begun to see the value in just trying to look at it for what it is, and what it is, is, I've got this ivy, and it is growing out of my asshole. I don't know why, perhaps I swallowed a seed or something, don't ask me why, I don't know, I never pictured this as a possible fate, I've never even heard of it before.

You can laugh, of course I can see the humor in it, I am not above laughing at myself. What I don't appreciate, however, is when people are unkind. Having been made the gift of several pairs of monogrammed garden shears, being called a "fertilizer eater," you can well imagine. The worst thing, though, are the gossips. Those with an insatiable curiosity about my dilemma, no sense of tact or discretion about it whatsoever. Asking me the most personal questions—and I don't even mind talking about it. I just want to be able to talk about it clearly, in a way that doesn't breed hysteria. You would be amazed, people asking me, "Is it kudzu?" and then stepping back as if they could catch it or something. It's not a disease, it's just something that happened.

The part of it that people do not seem to realize is that there is something...very...good...about it. People are very quick to see the inconvenience, the grotesquerie about it. And I'm the first one to admit it, I mean, it is ivy, and it is growing out of my asshole. That is grotesque. Without going into a detailed cataloguing of the ways it has changed the simplest things about my toilette: you can well imagine, there is a complication factor involved, there is mess involved; to be quite frank, I've found myself far more actively involved in my own shit than I ever thought I would be. But, it could be worse, it could be someone else's shit.

I've had to do some tinkering with my self-image: the shame, the fear, you can well imagine. I mean, if this is coming out of my asshole, god knows what is going on inside of my bowels. But I got over that, I didn't die, not yet, things are relatively, well I wouldn't say normal, but I am functioning. I did go through a period of the Job Syndrome, you know, what did I do to deserve this, what kind of test am I undergoing? The worst thing about that was trying so hard all the time to figure everything out. I would be wracking my brain, day after day, perhaps if I did this, or if I could go back and undo that, or if I make sure that I try extra hard to have these or those thoughts every single day, then maybe this situation would disappear. Well, that really led nowhere. I mean ultimately, no matter how hard I tried to do anything, the fact was, there was this ivy, and it was growing out of my asshole. Regardless of why it happened, or how I could have prevented it, the fact was, it was there.

So once I got to that point it was actually quite a relief. I started to become very curious about the manifestation of the thing. How fast did it grow, how thick was it, you can well imagine. That went on for a while, and then something happened that presented me with a far more provocative understanding of my situation. It had grown to a certain length, and it was just starting to trail out of the bottom of my trouser leg, and one day I was leaning against something and as I started to walk away, I realized that it had twined itself around that thing. I didn't think about it much then, I mean, that's what ivies do, they twine, so I just yanked it free, kinda, and went on. But it started happening more and more, and anytime I'd be anywhere for any length of time, it would happen. And after a while it started hanging on more tenaciously, and I'd really have to give it a yank. And sometimes it kind of hurt. But that didn't surprise me, I mean, it's a fucking pain in the ass, of course it's going to hurt.

Then one day it happened again, and before I could even think about yanking it free, I realized that it felt kind of good, being twined around that thing. I started getting these feelings that I hadn't had before, pleasurable feelings of warmth and... oh I don't know, it's hard to talk about, I mean, suffice it to say that they were feelings, and they were coming from that thing, traveling through the vine and into me. I mean, that is literally, baldly what it was like. And I am kind of ashamed to admit it now, but that really frightened me. I yanked it off really hard.

I spent the next few days restless and agitated, walking around, trying not to give it any more twining opportunities. And then I let my guard down and it happened again. And this time it didn't just feel good, it felt really great. But I yanked it off again. I don't really know why I did, I guess it made me uncomfortable, the idea of being attached up to something. I didn't want to get stuck there and not be able to walk away. But see, then it happened again, and this time it didn't just feel great, it felt really quite, right. Like I belonged twined up to that thing. So I stayed there for a very long time. It was very inconvenient, you can well imagine. But it seemed to be worth it.

But then the other day I woke up, in a panic. I realized that I'd been there for much too long. I didn't know what else was going on in the world or with any of my friends, so wrapped up had I been in this entwinement. So I tried to yank it free, and to my dismay, it wouldn't let go. Well I really yanked it pretty goddamned hard. But it was tenacious. I got more and more worked up, think about it, I could not get free! So I cut it off. With a pair of those gift shears. Well I don't want to talk about it, it was awful, I never want to have to go through that again.

So now I know what my options are. I can keep yanking it off, before it ever has a chance to get attached. Or I can keep moving around until I think I've found the thing, the situation, I could be attached to. But what if I'm wrong? Or I could just cut it off, right at the source, you know, go through the pain, survive it and get back to my life. But there's no guarantee that it won't just grow right back. So quite honestly, I don't know what to do. I mean, there is this ivy, and it is growing out of my asshole.

> (He continues to occasionally jerk his foot. The lights shift, and the performer goes and picks up a baseball bat that has been leaning on the side of the bed. Takes a hitter's stance, does some practice swings while speaking…)

Eight: The Willies

I'm ready…put it right here…right here…I'm ready for it…come on, here's my swing, here's my spot…right here…

I used to play baseball when I was a kid. Third base. That's a hard position you know. Really easy to get smashed by the ball. When it's coming off the end of one of those late swings, could have been a tipper, but the connection was made, coming at you hard and fast, right at your head…I was a good ball player. I never flinched. Lots of girls flinched. I would say that is one thing that characterized the difference between boys' and girls' baseball, to my observation. Girls flinched a lot more than boys. I know why. They really get it played up to them a lot about how much it hurts to get beaned. About how it would break your nose or leave ugly bruises and bumps that would never go down. I was lucky, I think. Right when I first started playing, the worst thing that could happen to a person happened to me. I got hit so hard the ball actually went right through me. It did. Right here. *(Points to chest)* It took off a piece of my heart. They didn't think I would live, much less play again, but I insisted. I figured, once the worst thing has happened to you, you're not afraid of it anymore.

We were playing in Fireman's Park across the street from my house. I was on third, and the teams were pretty evenly matched except for the coach. He was playing on the other team because they were one short. He was about 30, tall and strong, maybe he was somebody's dad, I don't know. He was trying to play down to our level, but it was obviously boring him, you could tell. He was messing with us a little, calling his hits but then bunting, stuff like that. It was kind of taking the fun out of it for me, because he was making us all self-conscious, saying things to us, like to one girl about how she jiggled when she ran. I started razzing him, you know how you do to the batter, and I may have said something a little harsh about him being "really good… against ten year old girls," but you know, I would have said it to anyone who was batting. He looked at me and fired a shot straight at me on the next pitch…When I came back to play the next year he was gone…

(Practicing the swing)
Put it right here…give it your best shot…
come on, I'm giving you my spot…lay it on me…

The experience gave me an advantage. When something is coming at you and you've learned not to flinch, you've got a better than average chance to have some control over the situation. I'm not saying bad things aren't going to happen to you, I'm just saying you have more control. It's a small point. It's been hard for me to get used to being a woman. I didn't get the implications of it until relatively late. Getting kicked out of the park when the boys were playing because I was a girl. Being cornered by Jim Dittberner behind the grove while the rest of the kids were playing red light green light. Being told by Kres Peckham in no uncertain terms that I didn't prettify myself enough for any boy to be seen liking me. My first exposure to the guys on the street's "ya-ya!" Being informed in detail about the way my breasts move under my shirt when I walk…I never ignored it, you know. At first I tried to reason with the construction workers because I thought if they understood how it made me feel bad, they wouldn't want to do it anymore. I tried that for a long time. Then I got tired of explaining my feelings.

The first time I didn't explain them, I was walking down the main drag in the middle of the afternoon. A group of five guys was walking towards me and as they passed, one pinched my ass. It pissed me off, so I turned around and kicked him in the ass. They all turned around and kicked me in the shins. I kicked back and soon we were having a kick fight, right in the middle of the sidewalk. No one stopped to help me, and I was starting to get hurt, so I kicked the nearest one hard in the balls. He went over. He puked. We all stopped for a second and it was obvious that the thing was about to escalate into something far, far worse. So the biggest, beefiest one, probably a poly-sci major, stuck out a hand and said, "Alright, let's just shake hands and call it straight." I was very angry and upset and I said, or rather yelled, "Why should I shake hands with you, you fucking no-necked beef faced bastard?"

He got really red in the face and became insistent and when I was clearly not going to do it, he said, "Shake my hand or you're a lezzie cunt." When I refused, this then turned into the worst insult he could possibly think of, "Shake my hand or you're an ugly lezzie cunt." I was so infuriated, I reared back and bellowed into his face a full minute of breath from a very garlicky lunch I had just eaten. He jumped back and protested, "I didn't touch her! I never touched her!" Nobody was giving a shit anyway. I can laugh about it now, it seems so innocent now…

Right here…right here…
come on I'm waiting…I'm ready for it…

I've been living alone. I really love it, it's good for me. The only problem is fear. Every night I go to sleep alone, I go to sleep afraid. Lots of nights I can't sleep. I get the willies. It's a jingly jangly energy traveling through my limbs. It comes from listening. I listen for every creak and flutter. I know what are my neighbors' footsteps on the stairs and what are not. I hung a pickle jar filled with pennies and marbles from the screen on my living room window. I thought that in the summer, when I have to have my window open, if someone messed around with the screen from the outside, touched it or tried to pull it out, I would hear the pennies and marbles in the jar making a lot of noise. I listen to the voices inside my head and outside my window. I'm haunted by the diatribes and laments and arguments, and by the possible fates I might suffer or that they might suffer. I've gotten so familiar with the cast of characters that carry on their personal tragedies in the alley in the middle of the night for everyone to hear, that sometimes I can't distinguish them from the ghosts that occupy my mind. Everyone who cares about me has said, "Why don't you move to a safer neighborhood?" I know they're fooling themselves. There are no safe neighborhoods anymore.

Sure I have a morbid imagination. That's why I became a writer. Just because I tend to imagine the most horrible things doesn't mean those things don't actually happen. On the street, I don't flinch. I can be an animal too. I can respond intuitively, without thought. But in my home, I'm more vulnerable. So I am prepared…

(Swinging bat, slowly, menacingly…)

I'm ready…I can hit it out of the park…
I'm ready…I can hit a home run…

*(Lights slowly fade on swinging bat stance…
Closing music of a lullaby, something peaceful, is played…)*

– *The End* –

Jenny Magnus & Beau O'Reilly in *The Trips*

The Trips: A Madras Parable

**Premiered 1996
Links Hall
Chicago, IL**

Performed by Beau O'Reilly and Jenny Magnus

SETTING

A bare stage. Traveling theme music starts. Heave Trip enters carrying a chair, puts it down and exits. Sop Trip enters from elsewhere, with a chair, puts it down, perhaps switching positions with the first chair, exits. Heave re-enters with a music stand, sees the two chairs, places the music stand, exits. Sop enters with a music stand, sees the setup, rejiggers it to a more suitable arrangement, and as Sop begins to sit down, Heave enters. They jockey for position and sit, Heave on the left, as a driver, Sop on the right. They sit in the chairs, Heave holding the music stand like a steering wheel.

Heave: (*Sings*)   Niagara Falls…

Sop: What more can be said?

Heave: (*Sings*)   Niagara Falls…

Sop: What more can be said?

Heave: (*Sings*)   Niagara Falls…

Sop: What more can be said?
        (*Pause*)

Heave: Well…

Sop: Yes…

Heave: Well, here we…

Sop: (*Interrupts*)   Yes, we're off, we're going.

Heave: What?

Sop: Going. Here we go.

Heave: Well, I was going to say, "Here we are," not "Here we go."

Sop: Oh, Ok… sorry.

Heave. That's alright.

Sop: (*Pause, as if looking at a map*)   Eden is on 75.

Heave: I'd rather go east of Eden.

Sop: Ok, that's on 391.

Heave: Huh.
(*Long pause*)

Heave: How long has it been?

Sop: For what?

Heave: Since we've started?

Sop: I don't know. Not terribly long. A little while. Why?

Heave: No reason. It just seems like it's been a little while.

Sop: It has been a little while. A <u>little</u> while.

Heave: Yeah, it feels like a little while.
(*Long pause*)

Heave: Want to do anything?

Sop: Ok.

Heave: Want to play "license plates"?

Sop: No.

Heave: How about "reading signs"?

Sop: Puke.

Heave: …"I dare ya"?

Sop: OK.

Heave: OK, "I dare ya." Hmm… I dare ya… to… not lie for a day.

Sop: Wait a minute, wait just a minute.

Heave:	What's the matter?
Sop:	What are you talking about, to not lie for a day?
Heave:	It's fairly simple, I think.
Sop:	Not lie like how?
Heave:	Like tell the truth.
Sop:	All day? Everything?
Heave:	Yeah, what's the big deal?
Sop:	It's kind of a big nut to crack, isn't it? Not lying all day long? Into the evening too? Or just til 5 o'clock or so?
Heave:	No, all, the entire day, until you go to bed.
Sop:	Well forget it, I can't.
Heave:	Really? You can't not lie just for one day?
Sop:	No.
Heave:	That's pretty lame, don't you think?
Sop:	Perhaps, but I know my limitations.
Heave:	That's an unacceptable limitation.
Sop:	What?!
Heave:	It's unacceptable. I mean this is basic stuff. Really. If you can't do this, then what can you do?
Sop:	What do you mean? I can do plenty. Plenty.
Heave:	Well, maybe, but what's it worth if you can't tell the truth about it?

Sop: What does it have to be worth?

Heave: What does anything have to be worth for that matter? All I'm saying is that it isn't even hard, to <u>not</u> do something. In fact, you don't have to <u>do</u> anything at all, just <u>don't</u> do something. Don't lie.

Sop: I guess I could do that if I just sat there all day and never moved and never said anything.

Heave: Well do that then.

Sop: What? Sit here all day and not move and not say anything?

Heave: Sure, plenty of people do that.

Sop: *(Incredulous)* They sit all day? And not move? And not say <u>anything</u>? *Deliberately?!*

Heave: Well, yes.

Sop: I can't do that. It would be like sitting in a rocking chair and not rocking.

Heave: It's interesting to me that you would find that hard. I wouldn't have guessed that about you.

Sop: Could you do it?

Heave: We're not talking about me.

Sop: Suppose we were.
Suppose I were to ask you something.

Heave: It would depend on what it is.

Sop: Why?

Heave: Because, there are just certain, well, taboos, you know,

	little taboodaleeoodaleeoos, things that we stay away from. If we know what's good for us.
Sop:	So what if I were, for example, to ask you about… say…
Heave:	This sounds dangerously close to a real question.
Sop:	No, no, hypothetically, if I were to mention a certain tendency you might have towards, say… obsesso-compulso-behavo…
Heave:	Uh uh uh… taboodaleeoodaleeoo.
Sop:	Or maybe defenso-irko-conclusion-leapo.
Heave:	Taboodaleeoodaleeoo!
Sop:	Paternalo-judgo-dumbo-gamo.
Heave:	Hey! *(Not kidding)* I said taboo. Shut case not open no discussing non conversation nix nuh uh.
Sop:	But wait a second. I don't see how come my character flaws and problems, gaping though they may be, are casual conversation material, while yours, possibly equally gaping, are not.
Heave:	Well if you can't perceive the obvious.
Sop:	…No, actually, I can't.
Heave:	I…I don't know what it is. It just is what it is. It just is.
Sop:	"It just is." It just is what?
Heave:	What it is, is…what it is, is… *(Sings)* What it is, is… what it is, is…what it is, is… It's…It's what it is, is… what it is, is, what it is, is it's…it's what it is, it's what it is, it's what it'll always be…

Sop: *(Interrupts, sings)*
Unless there's some things that you just don't know.

Heave: *(Harrumphy)* There's lots of things I don't know. Lots, that doesn't prove anything.

Sop: You can ask <u>me</u> something. Ask me anything, g'head.

Heave: Ask you anything?

Sop: At all.

Heave: Ask you anything?

Sop: G'head.

Heave: Ask you anything at all.

Sop: Ask me something hard. Ask me something tricky. Ask me something secret. Ask me something dangerous. Ask me something interesting. Ask me something ambiguous.

Heave: Something tricky? Ok, have you reached your ANTEPENULTIMATE MOMENT?

Sop: What?

Heave: Your ANTEPENULTIMATE MOMENT. Have you reached it?

Sop: Where does that leave you now, third to the end? That is a tricky position. You might never make it, know what I mean? You could always be trying, but you might never get to the end.

Heave: The ULTIMATE MOMENT? You might never get there?

Sop: Yes, you could get stuck. That could be bad. Never to get to the ULTIMATE MOMENT.

Heave: That's why I'm asking. As you get close to the ULTIMATE MOMENT it's good to be aware. So if you're aware of your ANTEPENULTIMATE MOMENTS, you know that there is only the PENULTIMATE MOMENT left between you and the ULTIMATE MOMENT. Have you reached it?

Sop: Oh, I don't know. I don't think about things like that. I think more about…Oh, you know what I think about.

Heave: No, I don't.

Sop: Yes, you do.

Heave: No, I actually don't.

Sop: Really?! You don't know what I think about?

Heave: No, like what are you thinking about right now?

Sop: Well, I'm thinking about how annoying I find it that you don't know what I'm thinking about.

Heave: Besides that.

Sop: Uh, I guess, I'm thinking about…all the way, open, now, totally, twice, it all.

Heave: What?

Sop: All the way, open, now, totally, twice, it all.

Heave: That's what you're thinking about?

Sop: Yes. So what?

Heave: Shouldn't you be thinking about, like, which way we're going, or how we are going to get there, or when?

Sop: I don't want to know which way we're going! That's your job. I just want to go.

Heave: Wow, I thought you were more directed than this. I guess I was wrong.

Sop: Yeah, maybe you were. I mean come on, I'm the scion of fears and negativity and confusion.

Heave: What about this "open" business? And "all the way"? All the way to what? How can you be open and all the way if you're the scion of fears and negativity and confusion?

Sop: I never said I was going to get there necessarily. I just said I was thinking about it.

Heave: I think you're confused.

Sop: Oh, I'm a very lowly creature. Honestly, I'm very worm-like. Didn't you know that about me?

Heave: No, I didn't.

Sop: No! No! It's true. I'm a base metal. My spine is as stiff as a rod. I am just like all the other people you've met. I want to kill you. Really. I want to kill you for your sense of direction. I'm angry and disgusted with myself, saddened. Low and high beings. That strikes me as very, very funny. What about sideways beings, where you aren't even traveling up and down but lodged sideways, blocking the path? And why am I having this conversation?

Heave: I couldn't say. But you're so passionate, such a hard worker. That counts for a great deal.

Sop: I'm not though. I'm a whiner. A cripple. I let everything get in my way. I let everything get in my way.

Heave: You said that twice.

Sop: For emphasis. I think too much and live far too little. If I could get somewhere I would've already. Look where you are. I'm like a piece of fruit nobody picked and I haven't even got the gumption to fall off the tree. And the worst thing is, right now, I don't even think it's funny.

(Heave, bored, stretches an arm across and, pointing at something, inadvertently puts it in front of Sop's face)

Sop: It's all dark, mutha dahling, I can't see!
Everything is obscure!
(Realizes it's Heave)   Oh, it's you.

Heave: First you want to kill me for my sense of direction, and now I'm obscuring your light? Pretty flippy floppy.

Sop: I don't really know what to think. Honestly, your whole presence has me in a muddle.

Heave: A dark muddle or a light one?

Sop: Up till now a light one.

Heave: I'd say go with that.

Sop: Yes, you would.

Heave: So go with the light. Don't get sucked into whatever.

Sop: Hey, it bugs me that you think you know so much.
I want you to comfort me.

Heave: Comfort you? Like what?

Sop: You know, like hold me like a child. Pat my head and tell me it's alright.

Heave: What if it's not alright?

Sop: Then tell me I'm alright.

Heave: What if I tell you you're not alright? That you're full of lies and bullshit, you're not at all what you seem, and you're manipulating me by wanting me to comfort you. What you want is someone to take on your pain and give it legitimacy.

Sop: Wow. You're not making me feel very much better.

Heave: Maybe you don't need to feel better.

Sop: This is low. Hitting me when I'm down.

Heave: Call me a cold fish, but I think it's a kind of pumped up hysteria.

Sop: You do?

Heave: Yes, and not what you really feel. What you really feel is…unattended to…unobserved. You want someone to witness your pain to ensure that it seems real.

Sop: It is real.

Heave: I think some of it is real. The rest is pumped up hysteria.

Sop: You <u>are</u> being a cold fish.

Heave: That is probably beside this particular point.

Sop: You think I would be suffering like this on purpose? Look how screwed up my face is.

(*Sop's face is absurdly screwed up.*)

Heave: You're an exhibitionist. In fact, when you really get upset, you try very hard to hide it.

Sop: That is only a little bit true!

Heave: I think it's true.

Sop: Well, I think you…don't care about me
and that's why you won't comfort me.

Heave: I care about you.
I just don't care about your dumb bullshit.

Sop: Don't put that on me!

Heave: What?

Sop: That image you have of me.
That weird and baseless
projection that isn't even me.

Heave: Well, if it isn't you, where did I get it?

Sop: You…invented it.

Heave: Out of the total blue?

Sop: Yes, completely baseless.

Heave: Not based on a single grain of truth.
At all.

Sop: Yes.

Heave: Then why did I make it up?

Sop: I don't know. Reasons of your own.

Heave: What possible reasons could I have though?

Sop: I don't know. Use your imagination.

Heave: But you've just been telling me not to
use my imagination.

Sop: About this projection.
Not about the reason for projecting it.

Heave: What if I told you that what you think is a projection is really the part of yourself that you want to be when you're around me?

Sop: You think I want to be like this?

Heave: Like what?

Sop: Cranky and difficult, stupid and dull, worried and fearful, paranoid.

Heave: That's how you think you're being?

Sop: Yeah, that's what I think.

Heave: Well my projection was that you were sincere and sweet, hopeful and earnest, effortful and candid, shiny.

Sop: Get out of here. That's what you think I've been like?

Heave: Yes, so if I've been projecting anything at all, it was that kind of thing. Not negative things.

Sop: Any projection is still a projection.

Heave: Oh…

(Heave disgustedly turns on radio to sports. Sop switches it, Heave switches it back, they duel. They futz with the car radio, using voices to do the different stations)

Sop: *(Contemptuously)* Sports.

(They futz, and finally light on a country station.)

(They both sing the following, or it is played, prerecorded)

Crazy (sung)

Spent the last few years in a panic of sorts
And just when I thought I'd calmed down
Something stupid
Something farcical happens
I've had all the keys in the palm of my hands
Nothing to pick up or put down
Then I lose my balance and I feel crazy
I feel like I'm crazy
Locked in a vestibule, what can I do?
Stuck between in and out, who'll rescue me who?
I can scream and cry I can rattle my cage
I can dare out all the gods to come down
Nothing happens, nothing happens at all
I can look outside at the world going by
And try to keep myself from slipping down
Then I lose my balance and I feel crazy
I feel like I'm crazy
Locked in a vestibule, what can I do?
Stuck between in and out, who'll rescue me who?
And how did I find myself here?
Well I wrote a song called why
And I sang it every day
I thought I'd made my point
I guess not…

Heave: *(Speaking again)* Want to pull over?

Sop: No.

Heave: Want to play "million questions"?

Sop: No.

Heave: Want to take some weird turn and get totally lost?

Sop: …OK.

The Trips: A Madras Parable

(They do, in fact, take a "weird" turn: they flail and make weird movements, physically weirding out...)

Heave: *(Once they settle, the speaking now in rhythms)*
...You are the imp of the perverse.

Sop: *(In rhythm, syncopated speech)*
I'm not the imp of the perverse.

Heave: Yes, you are the imp of the perverse.

Sop: No, I'm not the imp of the perverse. Imps are sylphs. I'm more zaftig.

Heave: Zaftig?

Sop: Yes, zaftig.

Heave: Like, not being humble? Or as in, not being lightweight?

Sop: Like, as, in, a broadening.

Heave: Well what about being nice or good?

Sop: What about being nice or good?

Heave: Nice or good? Nice or good, get it?

Sop: I think you've got something there. Yes, there's something that's there. A clear choice to make. In the name of the things. The things that are real.

Heave: There's something in sports...

Sop: In sports?

Heave: Yes, the sports have something that's real.

Sop: It's real.

Heave: Yes, it's real in the sense that it's sports. I find that the sense of the sport…appeals to something in me. It's as if the sport had a way, and that way was agreed, by all those involved, and they all took a part, and something occurred, by their efforts and wills, and an end was achieved, and something was won, clearly won.

Sop: *(Out of rhythm, back to normal speech)*
Clearly won is the thing.

Heave: The thing about sports.

Sop: Most things are not sports.
(Long pause)

Heave: I wonder how it is that you think things about a person, you think it's what they're like, but they're not really like that at all, they're like something you didn't think, you never thought of it, you thought something else, and then there it is, why did you ever think that first thing in the first place?

Sop: Like what? You thought I was together, that I had direction, but I don't and I'm not. You didn't realize that I was in reality a wicked evil rascal instead of a strong powerful super god.

Heave: Well, yes.

Sop: I think it's all about neatness.

Heave: Neatness?

Sop: Yes, like, how "it all" is tied together, a perfect little package, a present that one gives you, beautiful and neatly wrapped, only you don't open it right away, you'd rather savor it all neat, and then you notice something coming out of it, a fluid and a stink, something rotten in there? Perhaps you should have opened it right away at first, but you didn't and now it's a shock, a fluid and a stink. See what I mean?

Heave: I hear what you're saying…It's like being bewitched into disbelieving your instinct.

Sop: Actually it's more like wanting to be bewitched. But think how I feel about it. I mean, it's destroyed.

Heave: What?

Sop: I destroyed it.

Heave: What?

Sop: Your image of me. The weird and baseless projection. So I…I…I ought to be destroyed in return.

Heave: Hmmm…

Sop: Look, if I've got to be destroyed, I don't want to wait. Why don't you just do it?

Heave: Me, destroy you?

Sop: Yes.

Heave: No, I can't. I don't want to destroy anyone.

Sop: Well, if you won't and I've got to be, who the hell will?

Heave: You could destroy yourself.

Sop: Self-destruction? That's not really punishment is it?

Heave: Could be.

Sop: Would you recognize it as punishment?

Heave: I don't want to punish anyone.

Sop: You wouldn't be. You'd simply be recognizing my self-punishment.

Heave: Well how would you do it? Destroy yourself?

Sop: I could tell myself I hated my guts and give myself back everything I ever gave myself.

Heave: That doesn't seem like enough.

Sop: I could tell myself I never wanted to see myself again, scream at myself and get out of my life and run out on myself.

Heave: That seems kind of complex.

Sop: I could just give up on myself and never care about myself anymore.

Heave: Now we're getting somewhere.

Sop: Oh, why is it we live in a world where you can't pick your nose without paying through it?

Heave: Just be happy we live in a country where you can hail a bandleader without heiling a bundleader.

Sop: You <u>think</u> we do.

(Long pause)

Heave: I'm...I'm going to say something.

(Long pause)

Sop: *(After having waited for Heave to...)*
Well, go ahead. Say it.

Heave: I guess I can't just say it, like that, just go ahead and say it. I've got to rehearse it first.

Sop: Rehearse it?

Heave: Yes, I need to know how it's going to feel coming out, what to expect, and will it hurt, and how will it be received. I need to know all that so I am free to really be in it, to let loose.

Sop: You're not free to let loose unless you know how it's going to be?

Heave: Yes, because there are so many variables.

Sop: Ok. Well go ahead then. If you have to know.

Heave: I do. Ok, so you're there, and I'm here.

Sop: Right.

Heave: Good. Now I'll try a little and then you react.

Sop: Shall I be spontaneous?

Heave: No, this is my turn. OK, here I go. "Oh, you false vixen of perfection." *(No response)* Well?

Sop: Well what?

Heave: You didn't do anything.

Sop: That was it? I mean, I guess I was waiting for more.

Heave: More? Sort of like you need the flow to get into it?

Sop: *(Dryly)* Yeah, yeah, I need more…flow.

Heave: Ok, I can understand that. I'll try again. Ready?

(Said as a Tennessee Williams character)

"You false vixen of perfection…You've frustrated and deceived me for the last time! Now the tables have turned, they've turned with a vengeance…"

Emptiness (sung)

The tables turned
The way is clear
Now I've been burned
I have no fear
Not much is left
That I can see
The emptiness gets to me

My strength was weak
My hair was cut
I had no way
To crack a nut
I tried to run
I could not flee
The emptiness gets to me

I want what I want when I want it...

Some kind of mam
A style of sweet
I've got your hand
You're on my feet
I walked through fire
But recently
The emptiness gets to me

It's hopeless my dear, yes it is, it's hopeless...

Sop: I'm... sorry.

Heave: (*Long pause*)
That's it? That's how you're going to respond?

Sop: You sound disappointed.

Heave: Well, you have to admit that isn't very much.

Sop: What more could there be? When it comes right down to it?

Heave: You could defend yourself, and/or attack me back. I mean, can I be absolutely sure you won't do those things? Suppose we really do it, and I let loose and go for it, thinking you're just going to do nothing, and then in the heat of the moment you don't do nothing, you do something, well then I'm in a spot because I wasn't expecting it and I wouldn't be prepared.

Sop: First, I didn't do nothing. I said I was sorry.

Heave: Well pfff.

Sop: That's not a bit nothing.

Heave: It's a word.

Sop: That's all there is sometimes.

Heave: All that there is.

Sop: It's better than nothing.

Heave: Better.

Sop: Hey, I'm doing the best I can.

Heave: Well, it's kind of all potential and no delivery.

Sop: That's all there is. You've invented this bigger thing, this more that there isn't. You've invented this person who I am not, and now it's a disappointment that the invention was…an invention! I've gotta get out. I've got to go. I've checked the directions and now I've got to get out and go.

Heave: Got to go, huh? Got to get out and go. Well, how surprising. How novel and fresh.

Sop: That's a very sardonic tone you're taking with me. Don't you understand? It isn't my fault that I have to go. I just do. Can't you get that through your thick skull? What's the matter with you? Don't you believe in anything outside of your own experience? Isn't it possible that you just don't know what I'm talking about and so you want to think that it's nothing and make a big emotional deal out of it? Couldn't that be the truth of it? Huh?

Heave: Hit some tiny nerve, eh?

Sop: A nerve? What do you mean by that? Just because I know what I know doesn't mean that you can just tell me everything.

Heave: All I'm saying is that it seems awfully convenient to have to get out and go at this particular moment. A very convenient moment to be directed to get out and go.

Sop: Pure coincidence.

Heave: I can even accept that...and what's that you've got?

Sop: What do you mean, what have I got?

Heave: Something of _mine_ it seems like. It seems to me like you're getting out and going and taking something of _mine_ along with you.

Sop: I don't have anything of yours.

Heave: *(Pissed)* And what have we been doing? What has been happening here? Nothing of _mine_, well I must say that's some real nerve. That's some solid gall to say you have nothing of _mine_. How's about the little goofy Thursday laughs? Huh? Or the dog imitations? What about those? And I hardly think I need to mention the Leprechaun Dance!

The Trips: A Madras Parable

Sop: Well hum. Hum hum. What shall I say about this?

Heave: Oh, are you checking the direction as to how to get out and go away from this conversation now too?

Sop: No, I'm trying to figure out why you're asking me these things, what of yours I have, and whether or not I ought to stay and have this argument or get out and go. I mean, how come you always get to decide everything? How come I'm always just an actor in your movie? I want to be in the driver's seat for once. I want to make some decisions about how it's going between us!

Heave: Driver's seat, is it? Ok, fine. Be my guest.
(They exchange seats, muttering.)
Driver's seat... feels... kinda... different... doesn't it?

Sop: Yeah.
(Slightly unsure) It feels good. Yes this is what I want.
(Getting mumblier) Why should you always get to decide everything?

Heave: OK. So what's happening?
(Grandly) What shall we do? Where shall we go?

Sop: *(Very nervous about being in the driver's seat)*
Now hang on, let me get situated, I have to get oriented, it's all different on this side, it's a different perspective you know, I have to just figure out... what does this do?
(Whenever something is done, something happens, cause and effect. First, applies brakes.)

Heave: *(Breaks into weird immediate sobs)*
Why?why!why?why!

Sop: OK, let's not do that...Let's get scientific about this... if I do this and this, will we get...

Heave: *(Bitter, a consequence.)* Brilliant, see my nostrils flare? You're doing a fine job oh yes, quite in control, what's your next trick going to be, Mr. Driver's Seat?

Sop: No, that's not what we want. There's this…

Heave: *(Makes a terrible piteous grating noise, a noise like all the juice has gone out of the world.)*

Sop: Whoa!

Heave: This is kind of painful, being bandied about in this way. Being at your mercy, reacting all over the place.

Sop: Tell me about it. Look, you just come back over here, and do it. *(They switch back.)*

Heave: Ok, if I'm doing it, then I want some things changed around here. First, I want you to straighten up and fly right. Then, get your act together for taking it on the road, and do a bunch of other things I come up with whenever I come up with them.

Sop: I don't want to do any of that right now.

Heave: It needs to be done.

Sop: I don't want to do it now.

Heave: Why?

Sop: I don't feel like it right now. I'll do it later.

Heave: No, it needs to be done now.

Sop: Then you do it.

Heave: It's your job.

Sop: Then I'll do it later.

Heave: No, now.

Sop: No.

Heave: Now.

Sop & Heave: *(Chanted in a rhythm)*
No no…now now…no no…now now…*(Etc.)*

Heave: *(Realizing)* Oh, no! Oh great! We're lost! I've lost us!

Sop: Why are we veering around like this?

Heave: I've lost us! I've lost us!

Sop: You're being ridiculous.

Heave: *(Increasingly piteous)* Yes, as I've said, I've lost us, we're lost!

Sop: *(Slaps Heave)*

Heave: *(Slaps Sop)* We're headed for a crack up! We're going to crack up! We're cracking up!

(Screams, they get out and lay on the ground, not even necessarily falling, but ending up on the ground.)

Heave: We cracked up.

Sop: Yes, we did. We actually cracked up.

Heave: Are you alright?

Sop: Yes, I think so.

Heave: We're still here. We cracked up but we're still here.

Sop: We are still here. Here we are.

Heave: Why are we still here? I mean, we cracked up! This is a miracle or something.

Sop: It is not a miracle.

Heave: Then why are we still here?

Sop: It makes a better story, that's all, to crack up and still be here. I mean, crack ups, so what, there's millions of crack ups these days.

Heave: This is cracking me up! I mean we're still here. WE ARE STILL HERE.

(Looks at Heave, they look at each other and at the car.)

Heave: I'm sad to say, things aren't all that different.

Sop: Different from what?

Heave: From the way they've always been.

Sop: Did you expect them to be different?

Heave: I had my hopes up, I would say, halfway, but they were up enough to be up.

Sop: And things aren't that different?

Heave: No. In fact, they're chillingly the same.

Sop: The same as they've always been?

Heave: Yes, even though lots has changed. I mean, we cracked up, that's undeniable. No matter what happens now, we still would have cracked up. So I can't figure out why things aren't different.

Sop: Have you changed?

Heave: What?

Sop: Are you the same? Or different?

Heave: Sadly, I guess I'm the same as well.

Sop: That's the crux of it I think. If you haven't changed, how can you expect things to be different?
They'd kind of have to be the same, don't you think?

Heave: I see your point. So how do I do it? How do I change and get things to be different?

Sop: Have you ever asked yourself that question before?

Heave: Yes, lots of times. It's one of the things that hasn't changed.

Sop: That's a place to start. Look, should we, just, keep going?

Heave: Can we keep going, I mean, a crack up is a crack up.

Sop: Maybe we should pretend we didn't crack up.

Heave: No I'm against that.

Sop: Now that I'm thinking about it, I can't recall too many cases of "post-crack up continuance."

(They get up, check themselves out, look around…)

Heave: Really? Maybe it's just not done?

Sop: I feel at a terrible loss.

Heave: I do too, but the thing is, we're lost, that's why we feel at a loss.

Sop: I don't want it to be like this. I don't want to be here.

Heave: Neither do I. But we are here.

Sop: I would rather be…

(As they sing the following, they dance together, a formal foxtrotish kind of simple dance.)

Dreaming of a More Perfect You (sung)

Dreaming, dreaming…
Dreaming of a more perfect you
What was it that you said last night?
I think you mentioned something that I wanted to remember
But I was far away
You know you're often right to criticize me
I know I'm often criticizing you
But our feet are off the ground

If only I could take your qualities
And put them through the flames of a holy fire
I would jump in too
I know
This agony of hurt between us
Is never where we said we wanted to aspire
I can't stand it can you?
I know we're
Dreaming, dreaming…
Dreaming of a more perfect you…

(They finish dancing and look at each other. Has it solved anything? Probably not.)

Sop: Shall we leave all this here and just, go?

Heave: Leave all of it here? But it's everything, it's all that we have.

The Trips: A Madras Parable

Sop: I know, but we can get more.
Let's just leave it and go.

Heave: Ok, which way?

Sop: I don't know.

Heave: Want to take another weird turn?

Sop: Ok.

(They spin arbitrarily.)

Heave: I'm all dizzy now.

(Heave starts to clutch and grab at Sop.)

Sop: No, don't lean, you're pulling me down!

Heave: *(Falls)* Always putting yourself first.

Sop: I don't always put myself first.
Sometimes I do of course but not always.

Heave: You're putting yourself first right now.

Sop: Now? How can I be?
I'm not even doing anything right now.

Heave: You're not agreeing with me.
You're not admitting I'm right.

Sop: But are you right? I mean, you're not right.
So why should I be agreeing with you.

Heave: In order to put me first.

(They stand in silence looking at each other.)

Sop: Let's leave it and go.

Heave: Yes, let's just leave it and go.

(They walk side by side, exploring with flashlights, tentative, fragile. They take out flashlights and explore the space, looking for a way out, the lights fade to black.)

Sop: *(Sings)* Niagara Falls.

Heave: What more can be said?

Sop: Niagara Falls.

Heave: What more can be said?

Sop: Niagara Falls.

Heave: What more can be said?

Sop & Heave: Niagara Falls…

– *The End* –

Paul Leisen, Jenny Magnus & Beau O'Reilly in *The Lucky Ones*

The Lucky Ones

**Premiered 1999
The Lunar Cabaret
Chicago, IL**

**With Beau O'Reilly, Paul Leisen
and Jenny Magnus
Directed by Hallie Gordon**

THE
PLAYS

SETTING

Two people, of any age or gender, sit in lawn chairs on a grand sea of Astroturf. They are dressed all in white: a Victorian, elegant, detailed white, with straw hats and bare feet. A singer is hidden behind a wall of Astroturf behind them. The people are not aware of the singer, unless they want to be. The songs can also be pre-recorded, a little respite tableau when they play. The light is like a summer day, and throughout the play, the light becomes more like a blazing summer evening: gold, red, so intense you might have to squint your eyes if you looked into the sun, and then it dips down over the horizon, and all that's left is the afterglow... The "I don't want this" dialogue, spoken three times, could parallel this arc, from matter-of-fact to resistant to resigned, until <u>that</u> afterglow...

It's Really Ourselves We Mourn (sung)

Singer: Our ties to them are often brittle
Over those to whom we mattered little
It's really ourselves we mourn

Unseemly to fry up in a griddle
Over those to whom we mattered little
It's really ourselves we mourn

The first question is a trick question
To whom do we pay our regrets?
The blow we take is a blow we fake
Not even the body can hold our attention

'Kay 'kay okay okay 'kay 'kay' kay….

Older: I don't want this.

Younger: I know. I know you don't.

Older: I don't want this.

Younger: I know, I know.

Older: I don't. I don't want this.

Younger: I know. I know you don't. You don't want it.

Older: I don't want this. I don't want this.

Younger: I know you don't want it, but this is what it is.

Older: But I don't want it, I don't want it.

Younger: Yes, but this is what it is, this is it.

Older: But I don't want...

Younger: Yes, yes, you don't want this, you don't want it.

Older: No, I don't.

Younger: Yes, I know you don't.

Older: Do I have to have it?

Younger: Yes, you do have to. This is it.

Older: But do I have to have this?
Why do I have to have this?

Younger: Because this is it. This is what it is.

Older: This is...

Younger: This is what it is. This is all that there is. This is everything, every day, until it's over.

Older: When will that be?

Younger: I don't know.

Older: Will I know?

Younger: I don't know.

Older: ...I don't want this.

Singer: We are the lucky ones...

Younger: Well, it's soon. You're in trouble now.

Older: Yes, I guess so. It's soon.

Younger: You're going to have to go soon.

Older: I know it.

Younger: Have you finished? Or is it too late?

Older: I thought I might be able to finish but now I don't think so.

Younger: Did you try? To finish?

Older: Yes, of course I did. But these things take time.

Younger: Well, your time is running out.

Older: Yes I know.

Younger: Can anything be done?

Older: About going? No, I'm going, it's happening, that's clear, it's only a matter of time.

Younger: Can I do anything for you?

Older: Like what?

Younger: I don't know, like take care of things. Have you considered what to do?

Older: What can I do? My time is running out, I have to go soon, and if things aren't together, they aren't finished, well...

Younger: So what's to become of things? If they aren't finished? They can't just be left undone, can they?

Older: I don't know, I hadn't thought about it.

Younger: You'd better think about it. Your time is running out.

Older: What do you think I ought to do?

Younger: I don't know. What do you want to do?

Older: What do I want to do?
Hmmm…Shall I leave it to you?

Younger: To me?

Older: Yes, shall I leave it to you to finish things for me?

Younger: I don't know if I could finish things for you.

Older: I think you could. I don't know why you couldn't.

Younger: You really think I could finish things? What state are they in? How far are they from really being done?

Older: They're not quite nearly done.
There's some significant work left to do.

Younger: And you really think I could finish things?

Older: It would take work of course. You'd have to keep yourself from being distracted. But, yes, I think you could finish things.

Younger: I wouldn't get distracted.

Older: Well, you do get distracted. I've seen it.

Younger: No more distracted than you.

Older: Yes, but <u>my</u> time is almost up. <u>I'm</u> in trouble now. <u>I'm</u> going to have to go soon. That's an enormous distraction. I don't know who wouldn't be distracted by that.

Younger: Are you saying I'm <u>easily</u> distracted? More easily distracted than you?

Older: Let's just say that <u>your</u> time is not almost up, <u>you're</u> not in trouble now, and yet…

Younger: I'm not distracted.

Older: I'm not saying that you are.
I'm saying that you could be.

Younger: All right, enough of all that. Look, what's to be done?

Older: I told you. Things have to be taken care of. They have to be finished. And that's only the things that can be finished. And I'm asking you to finish them for me. If you can. Or will. Of the rest, of the rest, nothing can be done. Or rather, anything that can be done has already been done. If it hasn't been done, it couldn't have been done.

Younger: But <u>what</u> has been done? Has <u>anything</u> been done?

Older: What's been done is what could be done.

Younger: So it's all done? Other than the things that I could finish, other than the things that you think I could do, there is nothing left to be done? There is nothing more that I could do?

Older: Right. Nothing more that you could do.

Younger: Then, there's nothing more to be said about what's been done.

Older: All said, all done.

Younger: Because if there was anything...at all... to be said or done, I'd want to know... If I am going to say it or do it.

Older: There's nothing. It's all done.

Younger: Was it done by you? Were you the one to do it?

Older: Well, I said it…I said I would do it, but by the time I got to it, it had already been done, so actually I didn't do it, but it did get done. Don't worry about that, if it was there to do, it got done.

Younger: But not by you.

Older: Not by me, but it got done, nonetheless.

Younger: So who did it get done by? Who actually did it? If it did get done, and it wasn't you, you didn't do it, who did? How do you <u>know</u> it got done?

Older: It got done because there was nothing left to do. By the time I got to it, it was done. So I knew that someone did it because it was done. And once it was done, there was nothing left to say.
What could you say? It was done.

Younger: But who did it? If it wasn't you?

Older: I don't know.

Younger: You don't know who did it?
But you know it got done?

Older: Yes.

Younger: How do you know? How do you know anything was done at all? Maybe nothing was done at all! Maybe nothing at all was done and you just thought it was all done because it was all…

Older: I said it got done. That's how I know it.
Because I said it.

Younger: All you know about whether it got done or…or <u>anything</u> got done is that you said it? You said "it's done, it's all done, nothing more to do…"
and that was all?

Older: What more can be said? I said I would do it, but when I got to it, it was done, so I said, "it's all done. It's already done." It was self-evident to my reason, so I knew it was done.

Younger: In what way, exactly, was it self- evident to your reason? Did you see that it was done? Or just think it?

Older: I...let me think...I came to see if it was done... Because I had said I was going to do it... So then, when I came to see...

Younger: If it was done...

Older: Yes, if it was done...I said, "There is nothing more to be done." Yes, I said that.

Younger: Yes...

Older: Yes, and then, once I had said that, I saw that not only was there nothing more to be done, there was also nothing more to be said, because there was nothing more to be done. And then I thought, if there is truly nothing more to be done, then everything that could've been done would have already been done, and so again, there was nothing more to be said.

Younger: And so you based your entire assessment on what was to be done or said on that one statement of your own?

Older: One statement?

Younger: "Nothing more to be done."

Older: Yes, because there truly was. Nothing. More. To be done.

Younger: Yet we don't know if anything at all was even done. We only know, that according to you, there was nothing _more_ to be done.

Older: *(Done with this subject, looks at the waning light, wipes face, scratches head, speaks, perhaps as in a dream, perhaps as a soliloquy...Is this the answer? He does not know...The other person may or may not be hearing this.)*

There was...a sandy, scrub-like terrain, gritty under bare feet. Where are the shoes, they were on a minute ago, must have lost them, oh well. Don't like to feel the grit and thinking there might be bugs or fleas in the sand or a rock or something underneath lurking to hurt me or stub my toe. Broke a toe once stubbing and it hurt so bad it almost puked me. Walking along kind of confused and lonely, the kind of landscape that wants to be shared and commented upon, like "isn't that beautiful" or "where the hell are we." But just walking and gingerly trying to anticipate each step because there could be pain under it. Coming up to a big rock, a desert oasis kind of shade but it's shaped like a building, a carved from the elements building that even has indentations where the windows would be and the door-person is even hinted at, standing at his post just inside, waiting to swing open the suggested door. Don't want to go in there because even if it's hot and unpleasant outside it seems too dank and dim in there. Outside there is nothing hidden, all the bright light illuminates everything and the mystery is only where or when, not what. The rock is so perfectly sketched out and it's a miracle nature eroded it that way, even the pigeons roosting and gargoyles on the top. It is not pleasant to be alone, thinking of all past childhood friends, abandoning each one in their time, outgrowing them along with clothes and musical tastes. Saying the words "don't want to be your friend anymore" right to their faces and learning to hide the surge of joy and power from their looks back, crestfallen, angry confused or contemptuous. So then there aren't any friends here, a wave of regret hurting once it's all added up, where are they now, with other best friends, obviously. There isn't anything to do but stand there or move along, don't see anything else in the distance, this seems like the best bet but there is nothing good in the choice, only less bad. Wishing for a Coca-cola, not water, rather to taste the metallic poison at a time like this, what is there to save yourself for anymore. Don't care about clothes or the sandy stuff that gets into the ass crack. Plop it down and that's it. No one can make me move if I don't want to.

(Coming back into the scene)
Aaahhh, there isn't enough here to continue.
There's no point in continuing. Let's just cut it short.
It's better that way.

Younger: How can you say that? There's every reason to keep going. There are things, undone, unsaid, even if your time is running out, and you're in trouble now, I'm going to have to finish for you, the things that can be finished...

Older: No, no, you always say the same thing, continue, continue, regardless, continue. I say, it's already too late, I say, cut it short. Stop the hemorrhage.

Younger: You just said there wasn't enough to continue. How can there be a hemorrhage?

Older: What I said was let's cut it short. It's not enough, it's already too late.

Younger: If it's too late, let's let it go, let it rip, what the hell, if it's too late.

Older: No, I disagree. Let's cut the losses and stop now while we can.

Younger: Isn't it already too late?

Older: Yes, it's too late. In fact it's over. It's all over.

Younger: So there's nothing to stop really. Nothing to cut short. Let's just let go of the reigns and let it rip.
What the hell.

Older: No, we need to stop it. We can't just let it go and let it rip. We need to stop it.

Younger: If it's over why do we need to stop it?

Older: Look, in my opinion, once it's already too late, once it's all been said and done, once you've gotten someone to take care of the things that aren't finished, you've got to sometime just stop it.
For god's sake…You're pushing.

Younger: I'm not pushing.

Older: I can feel it. I can feel you pushing.

Younger: I'm not pushing. I'm easing.

Older: No, it's not easing. I feel pushed. It's pushing.

Younger: You feel pushed.

Older: Yes, I feel a pushing.

Younger: But you _feel_ pushed. Not eased.

Older: Definitely not eased. Pushed…Shoved, even.

Younger: You feel shoved?

Older: I feel something like a shove. It's a hard, quick push.

Younger: So not like a constant, steady pushing?

Older: No, more like a shove. Like a hard, quick shove.

Younger: Well, I'm not shoving. I'm easing.
So it's not me you feel pushing.

Older: Of course it's you. You're doing it.
There's no one else.

Younger: But I feel like I'm easing.

Older: Whether you feel like you're easing or not,
I feel shoved.

Younger: Well if I'm easing and you're feeling shoved,
then as far as I'm concerned, I'm easing and
you're feeling shoved.

Older: You can't be easing if I'm feeling shoved.

Younger: Well how can you feel shoved if I'm easing?

Older: All right never mind.

Younger: No, really, it's important-how can you feel shoved
if I'm easing?

Older: I don't know, I just do, I feel it.

Younger: But I'm not doing it.

Older: Are you saying I'm not feeling it?

Younger: I'm asking you to tell me, make me understand,
how you can feel pushed and shoved when I'm not
pushing or shoving, rather, I'm easing.

Older: I don't feel pushed and shoved. It's one shove, one
hard quick push, not a lot of pushing and shoving.

Younger: In any case, how can you feel one thing when I am
doing another?

Older: This is an impasse.

Younger: Yes.

Older: Well, whatever you're doing, just stop it. Easing, shoving, or pushing.

Younger: Are you sure you want me to stop it?

Older: Yes.

Younger: That leaves you with nothing, you know. Nothing to lean against.

Older: I don't want to lean.

Younger: You'll be completely free standing.

Older: That's what I want. To be free standing.

Younger: Nothing around you for miles. Not an ease or a shove in sight, just you, you and you, flapping about, free standing.

Older: Alright, fine, let me just do it then. My time, as I've said, is almost up…

Younger: Just realize that when I stop easing, that's it, everything will die down and settle and stretch out before you like an endless horizon of you.

Older: You're still pushing.

Younger: No, I'm easing. I just want to make sure you understand what we are really talking about here. I'd hate for you to suddenly find yourself, you know, free standing, without some idea of what's coming.

Older: …Well how bad could it be? To be free standing?

Younger: Nothing...whatever...to lean against. Completely...free...standing. No shove or push, not even a nudge.

Older: Yes, so?

Younger: What if it's difficult? What if it's tiring? What if you get stuck? What if you begin to want a little tap, a simple bump, to get you through it, but there won't be anything, will there? You'll be completely free standing.

Older: Are you sure this isn't pushing? I feel a little pushed.

Younger: You're the one who wants to be free standing. Not me.

Older: It's not that I want to be free standing. I just don't want to be pushed.

Younger: Didn't mean to push. I thought I would ease… I just thought this would lead nicely into that.

Older: It doesn't. It's not smooth or nice. It's awkward.

Younger: I really thought it would. Are you sure it doesn't?

Older: Yes, I'm sure. See it yourself. It's awkward.

Younger: Is that so bad?

Older: What do you mean?

Younger: It's being awkward?

Older: Well it certainly doesn't lead nicely.

Younger: No, but maybe that works. Maybe it's better that it's awkward.

Older: No, no.

Younger: Why not?

Older: Just think about it. It's awkward. There's a bump in it and it curves, then it's just all over the place and too much trouble. No, it's not elegant or smooth, it doesn't lead nicely.

Younger: Does it follow though?

Older: What?

Younger: Does it follow that it <u>must</u> lead nicely? Maybe the bump is better?

Older: No bump is ever better.

Younger: That's not true.

Older: Name me one bump that was better.

Younger: Well even if it isn't better, maybe it's just as good.

Older: No, no, that's all wrong. It's better if it leads nicely.
It's better if it's smooth and nice.
When it's all awkward it isn't better.
It's never better to be awkward.

Younger: Now that I cannot agree with.

Older: What?

Younger: Clearly it's sometimes better to be awkward. It's often better.

Older: That's absurd. Often better?

Younger: Well sometimes better.

(This begins as an answer within the conversation, and can become a stepping-out soliloquy, a companion to the first soliloquy.)

Younger: Say…walking along in the woods. Where the wind is blowing so tumultuously and hard like something's gonna happen something's gonna happen. Never does of course but that doesn't keep the incredible feeling of anticipation from making the woods seem exciting and romantic, like you're going to have sex with the woods any minute. Walking along and looking for something familiar because you've been here before, and you can never get back here by yourself, you came once with your brother and he of course knows the way, the way to all things exciting and mysterious and interesting and you never learn the way to those things, always along for the ride and not paying attention and then you try to get there yourself and there's no way for you to recreate the steps involved. But this day you're going to stay in the woods until you find that place you came to that one day, the place you'd bring someone special to if there was ever anyone special to bring, but since there hasn't been up to now you can't wait any longer and so you have to just find it for yourself. The rising feeling of this being a fool's errand is starting to be un-ignorable, but you keep walking and only allow the thought to ride along next to you, you won't pick it up and carry it. Then, just like in a perfect dream, you see something that looks familiar, a little place where the trees grow over the path and make an arbor, something to pass under, and it's so green and the light is actually dappled like it says in any book. You go under the arbor and down a steep place and there it is. The foundations of an old building, a hotel or something really huge, your brother thought it was a place where gangsters came to drink and fuck and make deals, but there's no way of knowing what it really was because it's just the stone perimeter and a basement and some outbuilding basements. But it's really large and it must be quite old because this woods has been a park or something like that for a long time, and this place has the feeling of being overlooked, like they would've ripped it out if they would have known it was here for anyone, a kid or and old person or a highly sensitive person, to stumble upon. It defines the whole landscape, like the woods, which were so all encompassing one second ago, are now dwarfed by the fact of this building having once been here. You walk around the building and feel strongly like this is your place and even though you were only there once before with your brother a long time ago, this place has your name on it, or its name is on you. You jump down into the basement and it's quite deep, at least 8 feet, and it's like being in a swimming pool with no water except it's all woodsy inside like the floor of the basement didn't hold up against the woods the way the walls did, and they've made their way in and there are even trees growing in there, it's that old. You have the feeling that you are in a place that you've been thinking about being in for your whole life, the surprise and relief that it's finally happening to you and you won't be excluded from the club of life anymore, that you are having an experience that is as important and interesting as anything else and that you'll leave here on this day knowing that if nothing else, you were here and that defines you forever. Then you realize that you can't just get back out of the basement, because the walls are all slippery and mossy and horrible, and you are so fucking stupid to have jumped down in there because you are in a pen of a kind, completely enclosed by these 8 or 10 foot walls, and the joke of it comes into your mind. All this time you thought only of getting here, getting back here, but you never thought of what you would do once you were here, unless there were someone with you to comment to or sigh with, which there wasn't once you did get back here, and now you are realizing that the experience of being here is one of terror because you're fucking stuck here and you thought you could just visit and revisit, but that was wrong. You're here to stay.

Older: (*Having listened to this*) …There's no way.

Younger: What do you mean?

Older: I'm not doing it. I don't think I can do it. I'm not going. I don't want it, I…

Younger: Don't give me that.

Older: I said I'm not.

Younger: What's the problem?

Older: There's no way.

Younger: Not one way? No way at all?

Older: No, not a single possible way.

Younger: I can't believe that.

Older: I'm telling you. It's true.

Younger: You're saying it, that doesn't make it true.

Older: It is.

Younger: You're saying that there is no way? Not that you simply won't.

Older: Yes. There is no way.

Younger: No way at all to do it regardless of your feelings about doing it?

Older: Yes.

Younger: And if I found a way?

Older: What?

Younger: If I found a way and proved to you there is a way?

Older: I'm still not doing it.

Younger: Ok, so there is a way. You just <u>won't</u> do it. You won't use that way.

Older: I don't believe there is a way.

Younger: I believe there is a way. And, I believe that you know there is a way, you just won't use that way.

Older: Are you saying I can do it, that I should?

Younger: I'm saying there is a way for you to do it. If you wanted to. To do it.

Older: I don't want it.

Younger: I know. I know you don't.

Older: I don't want this.

Younger: I know, I know.

Older: I don't. I don't want this.

Younger: I know. I know you don't. You don't want it.

Older: I don't want this. I don't want this.

Younger: I know you don't want it, but this is what it is.

Older: But I don't want it, I don't want it.

Younger: Yes, but this is what it is, this is it.

Older: But I don't want...

Younger: Yes, yes, you don't want this, you don't want it.

Older: No, I don't.

Younger: Yes, I know you don't.

Older: …Do I have to have it?

Younger: Yes, you do have to. This is it.

Older: But do I have to have this?
Why do I have to have this?

Younger: Because this is it. This is what it is.

Older: This is…

Younger: This is what it is. This is all that there is.
This is everything, every day, until it's over.

Older: When will that be?

Younger: I don't know.

Older: Will I know?

Younger: I don't know.

Older: …I don't want this.

Martyr (sung)

Singer: Shall (s)he be a Joan
A Socrates
And take the poison willingly
To burn him up?

By all means
Don't censor yourself, I'd rather that you played with me
Give me no fair warning, I want to be surprised
Just how will your trick come?
That is my game

> Do unto me
> We've seen the way you look when you have got the scent
> The calculations in your mind are putting math to shame
> I'll stick my finger in,
> It can't hurt long
> Shall I be a Joan
> A Socrates
> And take the poison willingly
> To burn me up?
>
> I thought I had no longer thought so...

Older: I can't stand it. It's almost time.

Younger: What? What can't you stand?

Older: The idea of missing anything.

Younger: Who said you're going to miss anything?
Nothing is going on.

Older: All of it goes on. With or without me.
I can't stand that idea.

Younger: Nothing is going on...

Older: No, I've never liked the idea that somewhere something was happening and I wasn't there for it. I'm missing it completely.

Younger: But you're not there, where the thing is happening, so you wouldn't know anyway.

Older: But I know it must be going on.
And I'd be missing it.

Younger: How do you even know it's going on?

Older: It's got to be. If this is going on,
then something else must be too.

Younger: How do you know? Not by the evidence of your senses. All of your senses are tied up here, so even if there is something going on somewhere else, you wouldn't experience it anyway, as long as you're here. As long as you're, you know, "here." So you're not missing it, because it couldn't be experienced anyway.

Older: …But I think about it going on.

Younger: Yes.

Older: And I wonder and imagine and worry about it.

Younger: Yes…

Older: I can hear about it. Or see reports.

Younger: OK…

Older: So doesn't all that prove it's going on and I'm missing it?

Younger: Yes, but what if that _is_ your experience of it?

Older: What?

Younger: You're experiencing it, if _that_ is your experience of it, so you can't be missing it. It's happening to you.

Older: But what if I'm not experiencing it?

Younger: How can you not experience it?
If it's happening to you?

Older: If I'm only thinking about experiencing it, not, you know, experiencing.

Younger: You are so….you…you _want_ everything. You want to dump your unfinished things off on me, and you want to be able to cut things short, knowing that you have to go, but then you also don't want it, you don't want it, even though you know you have to, and then you want to experience what you, I don't know, experience, and also you want to be assured that you won't be missing anything while you are experiencing the first bit...

Older: ...So what's wrong with that?

Younger: It's...demanding.

Older: It seems reasonable to me.

Younger: No, it's demanding. Is the whole of everything supposed to organize itself around you and your insatiable need for experience?

Older: I don't believe I have an insatiable need. I only don't want to miss anything.

Younger: Well why not?

Older: That seems obvious.

Younger: It's not. Why don't you want to miss anything?

Older: What if I'm questioned later? Or quizzed? About something I've missed? I won't know anything about it and I won't be able to answer.

Younger: So what?

Older: *(Long pause)*
Well, I've...I think I ought to be able to answer.

Younger: But I'm asking you. What if you can't?

Older: What if I can't answer?

Younger: Yes, if you're quizzed on, say, what you've missed, and you can't answer. Then what?

Older: Well, it would be bad.

Younger: How bad would it be?

Older: It could be the worst. I could be exposed and left to...

Younger: Exposed as what?

Older: ...As limited.

Younger: And so if in fact you are limited?

Older: I wouldn't like it.

Younger: But what would <u>happen</u>?

Older: Well, theoretically, I imagine I would... (*pause*) crumble.

Younger: Crumble?

Older: Yes, just dissolve and be...crumbled.

Younger: And....

Older: Then someone might have to come and sweep me up.

Younger: OK.

Older: Well, I would have to suffer the indignity of that.

Younger: Yes, you would have to experience that suffering.

Older: Yes. And then I would be, I suppose, viewed as nothing but a pile of crumble, and I would be quite hurt to be seen that way.

Younger: Let's stick to what would happen.

Older: Well, if I've been swept up, I imagine one does something with things that have been swept up, I'd be discarded, removed, and I can only imagine it going downhill from there.

Younger: Why?

Older: Why is it going downhill to be discarded? Because I want to be cherished up on a shelf, like a special knicker-knacker, a keepsake, from a treasured time, not thrown into a heap to be ignored and lost and forgotten.

Younger: But what if you were? Forgotten and ignored?

Older: No one wants to be forgotten and ignored.

Younger: I wouldn't mind.

Older: That is so untrue. You would mind.

Younger: No, I really wouldn't. It's the truth anyway. I am not memorable.

Older: This is false modesty.

Younger: No, really. What is so bad about being gone and missing everything and being forgotten?

Older: It's terrible.

Younger: But why?

Older: It makes it all seem so lonely, doesn't it? To be all alone, not remembered, or noticed, to know it's all going on after you're gone, it's so inelegant and…

Younger: *(Interrupting)*
Oh, that is the true reason it doesn't appeal!
Not to be alone or lost or forgotten, but that it is
"inelegant." Rather not how you pictured yourself.

Older: No, not a picture I prefer.

Younger: What picture do you prefer?

Older: I prefer to picture myself as graceful, even dignified.
That's very important.

Younger: Why?

Older: Why?! Because if I am to be discarded and
crumbled and swept away, at the very least
I prefer to crumble with dignity.

Younger: What if I told you that there is no such thing
as dignified crumbling. At least not in the
way you see it.

Older: How do you know how I see it?

Younger: I'll tell you. You imagine confronting the moment,
sighing your acquiescence, graciously agreeing
to become a pile, acknowledging your sweepers,
and perching in your lost heap with your pride intact,
at some deep dark level believing that you
are letting this happen, that if you wanted to,
you could stop it from happening,
but since you see the writing on the wall,
you'll go along, uncomplaining…

Older: All right. But if it helps me to imagine that I am
agreeing to my discarding, why isn't that…

Younger: *(Interrupting)* Because it has nothing to do with you! You're no more agreeing to it than one agrees with the weather. We simply acknowledge the weather, we adjust to the weather, but we can't imagine we have anything to <u>do</u> with the weather. You can't stave off the weather by telling yourself it's all right with you. Whether it's alright with you or not, whether the weather is…whether…

Older: It's nothing the same, nothing. Because I am capable of maintaining my dignity, keeping it intact when I go, when I am in trouble, and you are not, doesn't mean it isn't possible.

Younger: There is no such thing as intact. Once it's over.

Older: Well, we do not have to agree.

Younger: No, we don't.

Older: I think it makes you feel better to imagine that dignity is impossible because you believe that it gives you a different kind of dignity to believe that.

Younger: Well, yes.

Older: And so when you are lost and alone, and all you have is that brand of dignity, you will be able to comfort yourself with that.

Younger: Yes.

Older: So it is merely the kind of comfort we take that we disagree about, not the fact of needing to be comforted.

Younger: Alright, yes.

Older: Because one only seeks to cover oneself out of instinct, and if pride is an instinct for some, so be it.

Younger: …Why can't you just go?

Older: What?

Younger: Why can't you just give it up and go? Just forget about all of this, what you'll miss, and go. Just go.

Older: I don't…I don't want to go. I know I must but… I don't want to.

Younger: What difference does it make what you want?

Older: That's all I know. What I want. Or what I don't want. That's all I've ever thought about or known.

Younger: That's very limited.

Older: I know. This is just what I was saying.
It's so easy for you, to say all of this, to poke.
Your time is not almost up, you're not in trouble now…

Younger: You know you've got to go.

Older: …I know. I'll just miss everything…so much.

Younger: You won't even know it.

Older: I…I…I don't want it.

Younger: I know. I know you don't.

Older: I don't want this.

Younger: I know, I know.

Older: I don't. I don't want this.

Younger: I know. I know you don't. You don't want it.

Older: I don't want this. I don't want this.

Younger: I know you don't want it, but this is what it is.

Older: But I don't want it, I don't want it.

Younger: Yes, but this is what it is, this is it.

Older: But I don't want...

Younger: Yes, yes, you don't want this, you don't want it.

Older: No, I don't.

Younger: Yes, I know you don't.

Older: Do I have to have it?

Younger: Yes, you do have to. This is it.

Older: But do I have to have this?
Why do I have to have this?

Younger: Because this is it. This is what it is.

Older: This is...

Younger: This is what it is. This is all that there is.
This is everything, every day, until it's over.

Older: When will that be?

Younger: I don't know.

Older: Will I know?

Younger: I don't know.

Older: ...I don't want this.

Aren't We the Lucky Ones *(sung)*

Singer: A sunny day
A little play
So come what may
Aren't we the lucky ones?

A quickening note
The antidote
That's all she wrote
Aren't we the lucky ones?

The noble truth
Seems so uncouth
Who said that sooth
Aren't we the lucky ones?

So why why why why why why why…
Because because because because because….

– The End –

Amy Warren & Jenny Magnus in *The Strange*

The Strange

**Premiered 1998
The Lunar Cabaret
Chicago, IL**

**Performed by Amy Warren and Jenny Magnus
Directed by Eric Ziegenhagen**

SETTING

The set is a bedroom: there is a bed and a table with a lamp. The least amount of things necessary. It is the middle of the night. There should be a door on one side of the room and a window on the other. The characters are a woman, 30-50; and a girl, whose age in the play begins at 9 and advances toward perhaps 15.

One

(Offstage, loud cursing and noise, stumbling, crashing, the woman bursts through the door, she is obviously very terribly drunk, crying and a mess...
The girl is sleeping in the bed.)

Woman: *(Stumbling around in the dark...)*
Oh oh oh...oh oh no oh oh no...Fuck shit, ahhh...

Girl: *(Waking up, being surprised)*
Uhh, uhh, wha...wha...oh who wha...wha...
wha...oh who wha...Wha, are you, who is it?
You're making so much noise!

Woman: Oh, oh, oh no, no....Shit, fuck,
I can't believe this shit. This is it, this is totally...

Girl: What's the matter?
(Lights come up to reveal a little girl's room, she is in bed, woman is crouched on the floor.)
What's the matter with you?
Why are you making so much noise?

Woman: Just shut up kid, shut up and let me sit here.
I can't believe this...

Girl: What's the matter? What's the matter?

Woman: I pissed myself, OK, I was looking for the bathroom and I came in here and fucking pissed myself.
Satisfied? Now you know.

Girl: You...

Woman: I pissed myself.

Girl: You...

Woman: Pissed, pissed, like, peed? You know, not pooped but peed. Get it? Huh?! *(Crying, sloppy, angry.)*

(Pause)

Girl: Well, I've done that. That's not so bad.

Woman: *(Kind of stunned by that reasoning)* What the fuck! Well maybe it's not so bad for you, for a kid, but in my world, it is bad. It is not acceptable at all.

Girl: I don't think it's that important.

Woman: *(Pause)* You don't think it's that important?

Girl: No.

Woman: Well, I think it's important. I think it's...terrible. It's tragic. I don't want to be sitting here in my own piss in some strange kid's room.

Girl: Then why are you?

Woman: Because I couldn't find the bathroom, OK? I didn't know where the bathroom was, and I had to go really bad, ok? So I came in here and...

Girl: I get that. But why did you wait so long?

Woman: I don't know. I don't know. Probably because I didn't know where the bathroom was.

Girl: Are you drunk?

Woman: Yes, yes I'm drunk.

Girl: That's probably why you peed, then.

Woman: No, I peed because I couldn't find the bathroom. (*Beginning to get angrier at the kid. Why not blame her?*)

Girl: And you held it too long.

Woman: Yes! Yes, I held it too long, alright? Too long. OK? Now you know, it's all out in the open, you know everything about it, it's all clear, and you, little precocious fucking girl, can tell me everything about myself, right? Is that right?!

Girl: Why do you drink so much?

Woman: (*Embarrassed*) What? Why what?

Girl: Why do you drink so much? I mean, maybe, I don't know, but it seems like...

Woman: (*Harsh interruption*) You don't know, that's right, you don't know me well enough to be asking that kind of question.

Girl: I asked you because maybe that's why you peed, you know, if you drink too much, if you drank too much...

Woman: Look, yes, ok, I <u>drank</u> too much, but that doesn't mean I <u>drink</u> too much. Get the distinction? See the difference? I drank too much, I waited too long, and I couldn't find the bathroom, I came in here, and I woke you up. Now I'm sorry about it, and that's all I can say. You stupid fucking little kid.

Girl: Uh, uh, you're just... You're being really mean, you're not being very nice.

Woman: Well you're right. I am not nice. Not a nice person at all. And you don't have to think I'm nice, that's the beauty of it, see? I don't care. I cannot care, and not be nice, and you can just fuck off.

Girl: *(Freaked but belligerent)* You care. Everyone cares.

Woman: No, I don't fucking care. *(To self)* I don't want to care. And I don't want to want to care.

Girl: I think everybody cares. I think you care.
And I think you want to care.

Woman: I don't want to, I won't, I can't.

Girl: *(Getting into the game of it)* You could.

Woman: But I won't.

Girl: But you could. Admit you could.

Woman: I could, I could, but I won't.

Girl: You could! You said you could!

Woman: But I won't. So what? I don't. That's the point, I don't.

Girl: But you could. You said you could. You did.

Woman: But I don't. So I won't.

Girl: You don't, so you won't?
Isn't it you won't, so you don't?

Woman: No! I just don't, so I just won't. I don't want to, I won't. *(Fed up with the game)* Look, I'm tired. I'm so tired. I'm really very exhausted.

Girl: It is the middle of the night.

Woman: *(Sickishly)* Oh, oh, oh no...I really feel like I have to lie down. Can I just lie on the edge of your bed? I won't bother you, you just go back to sleep.

(The woman climbs painfully into the bed.)

Girl: Uh, uh, wha...what...I...don't think I can if you...

Woman: No, it's OK, I just have to sleep for a little while. I'm just going to get on the bed, just a tiny corner, for a little while...

(The girl is very uncomfortable and gets out, kind of ejected from the now horrible bed.)

Girl: Look, you just go ahead, I'll just sit up, I'm awake now, it's OK...

(She walks over to where the woman was, and watches the woman, saying things experimentally.)

Ulh...ulh...oooulh...You're ugly...You stink...I'm not impressed by you....I don't like your clothes...I'd be embarrassed if I were you...It's not important. I wasn't sleeping anyway. I was only pretending to sleep.... You make me sick. People like you make me sick. I think that's the worst thing you can do, is let yourself get stupid. Embarrass yourself and not even be able to stop it. Ulh...ulh...

Woman: *(Responding from bed)* I'm not sleeping.

Girl: *(Startled)* Uh...oh...I thought you were. Asleep.

Woman: No, I wasn't. I'm not. I just let you think I was. I wanted to see what you'd do. If you thought I was sleeping.

Girl: Why? Why would you want to do that?

Woman: Because I'm not nice. And to satisfy my curiosity.

Girl: About what?

Woman: About you. *(Meanly trying to freak her out)*

Girl: Why? Wha...uh...Why are you curious about me?
I'm not interesting.
I'm just nobody. Leave me alone.

Woman: Yeah, you didn't surprise me.

Girl: I didn't surprise you? *(Kind of insulted)*

Woman: Do you think I didn't know exactly what
you would do?

Girl: How could you know what I was going to do?

Woman: ...You remind me of myself.

Girl: Well I'm not going to end up peeing in my pants in some kid's bedroom who I don't even know.

Woman: Oh, oh ho, you just hold on to that thought.
Hold on tight. You just hope for yourself that isn't going to happen.

Girl: Just because bad things happen to you doesn't mean that's the way it's going to be for everybody.
I'm not going to feel all sorry for myself
and be pathetic.

Woman: You think I'm pathetic.

Girl: Yes, I do. It's embarrassing for a kid to see an adult all ugly and weird. If you were another kid I would make fun of you for being so stupid and ugly...Kids don't let kids get away with...

Woman: …Look, it doesn't really matter, but you are making fun of me. You don't think you are but what you're saying is actually worse than if you just laughed right in my face.

Girl: I don't get that.

Woman: *(Kind of sick of it now)* You don't get a lot of things.

Girl: Do you have any kids?

Woman: *(Surprised, laughing)* Uh, no.

Girl: What's so funny about that question?

Woman: *(Very bitter)* Do I seem like someone who has kids?

Girl: I don't know. All kinds of people have kids. Really strange people have kids.

Woman: You're saying I'm really strange.

Girl: I think you're kind of strange…
But I like things that are strange.
And you're not so strange you wouldn't have kids maybe.

Woman: Well no, I don't have any kids.

Girl: Do you want to have them?

Woman: I don't choose to have them. Not now.
If, in the future, I choose to have them, then…

Girl: I wish I could choose things. No one telling you all the time to do things you don't want to do.

Woman: At the same time, it's all up to you.
No one has to care about you.

Girl: (*Pause*) You know what, my mother has two pairs of glasses. One that she wears with black or white clothes, one that she wears with earth colors. I think that is too much.

Woman: (*Another bizarre non sequitur. The woman is struggling to keep up.*) What are you talking about now? Two is too much?

Girl: Yeah. It seems too planned out. Like she knows exactly what kind of occasion everything is going to be, and has just the right face to meet it with.

Woman: That seems alright to me. It's only some glasses.

Girl: No, it's not only the glasses. It's the plan.

Woman: What's wrong with a plan?
Maybe it gives her comfort.

Girl: It gives her protection, not comfort.

Woman: So what? What do you care if she feels better with…

Girl: Not better. Safer.
She feels safer with the right glasses.

Woman: Why begrudge her safety?

Girl: I never see her face then. She's so safe she's invisible. Her glasses give her a face. Maybe she doesn't have any face under there.

Woman: She has a face. It's her face. If she wants to only show it to the mirror it's none of your business.

Girl: When I was a baby in her arms I would try to pull them off. You know what? I never could.

Woman: That's not a real memory.

Girl: Maybe not, but that's my dream of the memory. That is the memory I think about.

Woman: I don't believe in that. Leave it all well enough alone, that's what I think. Don't mess around with that stuff, leave it where it lays, let it fester and rot all by itself. It doesn't need any stirring up by anybody. There are things it's better to not know.

Girl: I want to know.

Woman: You already know everything you need to know.

Girl: No, I don't.

Woman: What do you think you don't know?

Girl: I know I don't know enough.

Woman: Then that's all you need to know.

Girl: I want to know more than that.

Woman: Wanting, needing. Different things.

Girl: I need to know about wanting, then. Because I don't...

Woman: You do not need to know about wanting. Maybe you want to know. But need? Need is breathing. Sleeping, shitting. Wanting is all the rest.

Girl: How sure are you about all this?

Woman: I'm a scholar of want. I have a library, many volumes on wanting. All in my head, memorized. I know the difference.

Girl: That's fine for you, but...

Woman: No, we're the same. Everyone is just the same.

Girl: I don't think you're right.

Woman: You don't have to think so.

Girl: …I don't think you try hard enough.

Woman: Hard enough for what?

Girl: To feel better. I think you give up too easy.

Woman: *(Quietly. Has it hit home?)* I could hate you for saying that.

Girl: Why?! Why could you hate me? I'm just saying…

Woman: It's so wrong. It's wrong to think that just by trying harder I could somehow feel better. This is a part of me. Feeling this way is what I am. This is, for me, like the color of your eyes or something. It's not something I'm doing. It's just me.

Girl: You talked yourself into that.

Woman: No, this is from years of rational observation and experiment. I've been conducting a series of experiments, an elaborate process of elimination. I've removed every single external source of pain in my life, I've narrowed my life down until it's tiny, do you understand me? It's smaller than anything you could even imagine, like a matchbox life, but the pain is still there. Therefore, I conclude, I am the pain. Like, I saw my mother once, in a dream. She had had some dental work done on her front teeth. Where they had been chicklety before, capped, I suppose, now they were just stumps, hurting, blackish. Her eyes had all this pain. Not just mouth pain of the dental variety, but sorrow and shame.

Especially shame, like it was a hideous thing for her, a disfigurement that she couldn't abide. A loss of dignity. I felt so sorry. That's the kind of pain I'm talking about.

Girl: I don't have to believe that story.

Woman: Believe whatever you want to believe.

Girl: I think it's sort of ridiculous.

Woman: Yes, I would have to agree.

Girl: As if you couldn't change. Everything can change. At any moment. Even I know that.

Woman: Everything can change, yes, I know that is true.

Girl: So you can change.

Woman: Yes, but I can change for the worse. Or hadn't you thought of that?

Girl: Oh you make me so mad. Coming in here with your ideas. It's just ugly, you know? It's ugly what you say. And depressing.

Woman: That's right. You think you can stave off everything bad and ugly just by, what, looking at it straight? I give you points for not being a freakout kind of kid, like many would be, this is a bad situation, but you're still stupid and I'm not sorry to tell you that. Ugliness. Failure. Disappointment. You have no idea, kid, really, listen to me now, no idea what real disappointment is. That something is not ever going to happen. Ever. Sometimes it's not your fault, but when it is, when you've fucked things up and they're ruined, it's more than you can bear. It's more that I can bear. Someday you'll thank me for telling you this stuff. I don't care about you enough to sugar coat it for you. You think this is just some crazy woman talking talking talking. But ugliness is real, kid, it's all around you, all the time, and it's inside you, yeah even you, and it can come out. Just because it wants to. Just because for the hello of it. And then you can get used to it, you can start liking the ugliness, and you want to see how far you can go with it. Like right now. I just feel ugly. It's coming out of me. And you're the only person here with me. See how ugly I am?

(She grabs the girl and drags her to the bed. She turns out the light, does something violent to the girl. The audience cannot see what it is but they know it is something horrible. The girl stumbles out of bed, getting away from the unnamed violence. She hastens to the other side of the room, breathing heavily, collecting herself. A horrible pause.)

Girl: *(Finally, erupting)* Uh... I don't care what you say. You think you're scaring me but you're not. I can take it. I won't give up. I won't. I'm not going to get all ugly and flat and disappointed, and...

Woman: Fine, great. You're wrong, you will, but you just keep dreaming. Go to sleep now. I'm sorry I disturbed you. Just forget we ever talked. Forget about me. Do whatever you want. Go back to sleep. *(Stumbles out.)*

Two

(Some time has passed, but the girl is still quite young. She is seen climbing in through the window. It is obviously late at night or early morning, and she is sneaking back into her room from having been out.)

Girl: *(Angry, drunk, falling down, making noise)*
Oh, oh, no...

Woman: *(In the bed, being awakened by girl climbing in window.)* Wha, uh...Who is it?

Girl: What the fuck?! Who is it!!? This is...oh man this is just great, I can't believe this shit...someone in my room, fucking bullshit... *(She is kind of trying to be quiet.)*

Woman: What's going on? What are you doing here?
Who are you?

Girl: Who am I? That's funny, who the fuck are you?
What are you doing in here? *(Looks closer)*
Oh my god! What are you doing here?!

Woman: What am I doing here? What are you doing here?
Who are you?

Girl: Fuck you. Get out of my bed.

Woman: Your bed?

Girl: Yeah, this is my bed. So get out.

Woman: You're drunk.

Girl: So what?! So what if I'm drunk, what do you care?
Who are you to...

Woman: What are you talking about?
Calm down now, keep your voice down.

Girl: Yeah right, don't want any trouble.
Get out of my bed and there won't be any trouble.

Woman: There's not going to be any trouble.
Calm down now, just be quiet.

Girl: Stop talking. Just stop even talking to me and get out of my bed.

Woman: Are you...

Girl: Yes, it's my bed, my fucking bed, I'm kicked out but that doesn't mean it's not still my bed. It's my bed until I say it isn't, till I quit this room, not when I'm told to get out. I tell who to get out. I tell you to get out, you don't tell me! *(Crying, angry, losing her shit)*

Woman: *(Taking charge)* Look, shut up. Shut up and sit down. Here, I'm out of the bed, alright? OK? I'm up and out of the bed, now shut up and calm down.

Girl: Ok that's what I want. Move away, go over there, go out, leave me alone now, I just want to sleep. Get out and don't say anything more.

(She stumbles into the bed.)

Woman: Alright fine, quiet now.

(She watches the girl lay down, speaking to herself.)

This is terrific. What did I expect. Oh well, they never said it would be easy. I guess it's perfect really.
An uncomfortable evening and an awful night.
What do I expect. Creepy.
Little strange asshole angry kid.

Girl: *(Not sleeping)* Can't you ever shut up?

Woman: I thought you were passed out. Sorry.

Girl: Ha! Sorry!? You're not sorry. It's some kind of thing with you. Disturbing my sleep. This is like some bizarre nightmare, finding you here. It's like a little reunion. *(Finds that drunkenly funny.)*

Woman: A reunion? What does that mean?

Girl: You know what I mean. It's only justice that I should wake you up. Tit for tat.

Woman: I don't know what you're talking about.

Girl: Yes you fucking do. Don't be so stupid.
You woke me up, so I'm waking you up.

Woman: I didn't wake you up… You woke me up.

Girl Not now. Before.

Woman: Before? When?

Girl: *(Dawning)* Oh my fucking god.
You don't remember me, do you?
You don't even remember me.
You don't remember me.

Woman: Ok, I get that you think we've met, but we haven't. *(Very uncomfortable)* No, we haven't met. I don't remember meeting you. No.

Girl: You don't remember me. This is too funny. *(It's not funny at all.)* You don't even remember me at all? Look at me.

Woman: No, I'm sorry. I don't recognize you, look, I'm only here for this one night. I've only been here once before, to this house once before, but I've never been in here and I've never seen you. I don't think.

Girl: That's right, you don't think, you just come in here and wake people up and tell them things and freak them out, and, other things, and then you go. Is this going to be like, a ritual or something? Your drunken fucking vacation visit?

(Woman starts to come over to her)

Don't touch me! Stay over there, I mean it! I'll kill you if you touch me again.

Woman: I haven't touched you, calm down. Sshh.

Girl: You don't remember meeting me but you know you haven't touched me. Fucking asshole.

Woman: I came here to tell them I was sorry because I... of something, some things I did when I was here before, and it got too late to leave so they put me up in here for the night, one night, and that's all there is to it.

Girl: No, that's not all there is to it. Whether you remember me or not, whatever you did down there, to them, you did come up in here and you did fuck with me, you did, and whether you know it or not, I know it, you woke me up and you fucked with me.

Woman: *(Giving in to it)* Ok, ok, I can't remember. This is so horrible and creepy. Ulh... What, what did I do? What did I do to you? Just tell me straight out.

Girl: You fucked with me, man. With my mind. You... upset me and scared me and you... it's like you wrecked me, you came in here and just, infected me with some kind of poison. And you did shit to me... scared me and you freaked me out! You confused me and, it's like, I was really sure about things before that, before you, but then I got very confused and everything turned to shit. It all turned to shit and it's your fault.

Woman: *(Now very terribly upset)* Oh god, I am so, so sorry. I did shit to you? What possible reason could I have had for doing that? I am so sorry, I don't remember

	anything, I was drunk and I came back to make it up to them, for what I did to them, but I don't even, I didn't even remember that I came in here, and now you say I did shit to you? Oh god this is the worst thing I've ever done, I am so sorry.
Girl:	It's too late to be sorry, asshole. You already fucked me. I'm already fucked. Being sorry doesn't change anything.
Woman:	How can I tell you? I've changed. I'm not the same. That's why I'm sorry, I wouldn't be sorry if I hadn't changed. I never used to be sorry, I didn't even know I needed to be sorry, but now I do know, and I know it can't always be made right, but…
Girl:	That's right, this is one of the times it can't be made right. It's wrong, what you did was wrong, and what you're doing now is wrong. So just shut up and get out.
Woman:	Wait, wait…I can't just leave until we talk this out, what exactly happened? Just tell me what I did so at least I know. I can't do anything, I can't change anything if I don't know what it is, I have to see it before I can change it.
Girl:	You're not listening to me! I don't care if you change or not. You're right, though, you haven't changed, you're still just interested in yourself, yourself, yourself. You were, at least you were strange before, now you're just pathetic and weak and ugly… *(Taunting her, throwing insults)*
Woman:	*(Grabbing her, losing her temper)* Tell me what I did!
Girl:	Let go of me!

(They fight, the woman wins. She pins the girl on the bed, her knees on the girl's arms. They are face to face.)

Girl: OK, fine, you win, fuck you, I don't care.
(Crying, drunk, sickish)

Woman: Now tell me what I did to you. Exactly.

Girl: *(Not willing to really tell it)*
You did shit to me, no big fucking deal.

Woman: I did shit to you. Why?

Girl: Because you were drunk and you got mad.

Woman: And that was why you freaked out?

Girl: Actually, no. I freaked out because you…disgusted me. You were totally disgusting and filthy, you pissed yourself and cried and everything, but what made it weird is that you made sense. You were totally fucked up but you were right. You told me that I would see it your way, and learn when I got older and you were right. I did learn. Things can happen for the worse and some things can happen that can never be undone. I started thinking about this girl I know, in school, and this year, in one year, these terrible things started happening to her, she went to the bathroom and tucked her skirt into her underpants and walked around like that all day and no one told her. I didn't even tell her. Then her front tooth just turned black and died, and she just had this black tooth. Then she washed her hair with baby oil instead of baby shampoo one morning and it stayed wet and stringy all day. Then she gained like 100 pounds. Then she accidently yanked a chunk of hair out of her head and it grew back in curly, even though her hair was straight, so she had this one curly lump on her head. And her father started fucking her, she told me, all this happened, and she was so scared, like why? And none of it could ever be undone. I saw what you said, things can change for the worse, and even if you wouldn't have said all of that stuff if you hadn't been fucked up, because no one tells you anything real, I know that, you told me the truth, and...

Woman: Wait, now, I told you a truth. Maybe. Or some truths. But not the truth, the one and only truth that is always true. Because I want to tell you now that what I want to tell you now is also true. I just didn't know this truth at the time. Another truth is that even if you can't change something that has already happened, you can change yourself. You can make reparation and restitution, and make up somehow for what you've done. It's not easy, and I hate it, but you can, if you're willing to...

Girl: I don't believe you. You're just scared, or...
You did tell me the truth, you can't make things right. Once it goes sour, you can't make it right.

Woman: I want to make things all right again.

Girl: Was it ever all right to begin with? What if it never was? How can you know if it's right again,
how do you even think you can know?

Woman: You make it up, I guess, I've just figured out some way or made up some vision of what right is, or would be.

Girl: Well that's just terribly inspiring.

Woman: OK, fine, you don't have to forgive me, I know that.

Girl: Oh, oh, forgive you—I'm supposed to forgive you? Did they forgive you? *(Pointing downstairs)*

Woman: Actually, no. Not really.

Girl: Well, you're just doing great. You carry this infection around and expose everyone to it and then you want to be forgiven for that. You should just stay by yourself and keep this to yourself.

Woman: *(Very tired and horrified and drained)* Ah shit...
I was having this dream, when you came in. You woke me up out of this strange dream. I dreamt of being in some kind of union insurrection at a hospital or compound. I get into the compound very easily and I'm not suspect at all, it is extremely packed with people. Suddenly a door opens and out comes the main man of the place, obviously a figure of immense power and insanity, or worse, everyone is brainwashed, it's obvious all of a sudden, they can't take their eyes off of him, and they are all drinking what looks like carrot juice from a to-go cup with straws. He rolls out, and I am very scared of him, he is tremendously fat and unspeakably ugly, weird beige skin and no hair really, or like it's brushed back, but huge white teeth as the main feature, his eyes are psychotic, unfocused, and as he keeps moving it seems like the crowd is rolling him because he is moving very smoothly for a man his size. His back is to me, I hear someone say very proprietarily, "Isn't that cute?" and I look down to see and it's that his pants have only the tiniest amount of leg separation, just at the bottom and it occurs to me that he's mutated and has some kind of tail or something underneath those pants. Then he is passing me and mercifully his eyes don't light on me or notice me in any way but just keep blank and he is enveloped into the room he came out of. I am revolted and back out of the room. I stumble into this basement room and I'm in a cage or a cell with an obviously imprisoned woman. The floors and walls are metal but weirdly inscribed or scribbled on or into, and she is very short and slight with short hair. She kind of reminded me of you. She is naked and maniacally angry, like she's imprisoned down there because she won't obey, but lucid. Somehow we connect, she can tell that I am incognito or that I respect her anarchy, and she shows me her level of regression or defiance

or freedom or degradation by menstruating on the floor, obviously having no sanitary facilities. She just looks into my face and squats a little and forces out some blood, she is laughing, enjoying my despair for her. I decide to get the hell out so I can help her by destroying this infernal place. I leave and a guard sees me and I mutter about how she could be so vile, she is considered unspeakable by them. I'm trying to leave the compound and suddenly there is a pursuit, like I've been found out, so I drop onto all fours to move faster, pulling at the ground. I think I'm making it, and I see a strip of sand on the other side of the street and I think that's outside of their jurisdiction. I pull myself onto the sand, it's very difficult, but just then, a Jeep with some blond surfers in it pulls up and tells me that the real safety is still further on, at the window of a building ahead, that is where the real safety is, and I start trying to get to that, and that's when you came in through the window and woke me up.

(The woman realizes the girl has fallen asleep while she was talking. She sighs, oh, oh, and gets up and leaves, going out the door.)

Three

(Woman quietly sneaking in through the door while girl is in bed sleeping, woman watches girl very quietly, sits on edge of bed and touches girl lightly, to awaken her.)

Woman: Uhh, umm...

Girl: *(Without moving)* It's you, isn't it.

Woman: Yes.

Girl: I was having an illicit party in my house....

Woman: Listen, I came to tell you something.

Girl: *(Out of a dream)* No, listen, I was having an illicit party in my house, like the folks were gone, and I had people over, and someone had taken a piece of wood out of the fireplace and thrown it on the floor, and melted the rug, no fire had started, but the rug was pocked with these melted places, and I got horribly angry, like worse than I ever get in real life even, at how stupid someone was, how thoughtless. So I picked the wood up and under it, I saw one of the holes was really deep, like a crater actually, a crater in the rug, and at the bottom, there was not a door exactly but somehow I knew I should climb down the crater, so I did, and I found that under the floor, there was an exact replica of the whole house, like they had built two right on top of each other, but an exact replica, like even the furniture was the same and the knicker knackers, and everything, except it was subterranean, and kind of blueish, like a secret other version of their world under the actual one. I was walking around in the blueishness, touching things and picking them up, everything was the same, even magazines on the table. Weird, huh?

Woman: *(Not really that interested)* Yeah, I wanted to say, well, I guess, so long, or whatever, I wanted to see if you would be here, I didn't really know. I'm glad you are. Back here.

Girl: Do they know you're up here?

Woman: No.

Girl: How'd you get in?

Woman: I snuck in. I didn't need to see them.

Girl: Why did you want to see me?

Woman: I just wanted to. To see if you'd be back here.
I couldn't get you out of my mind.
I just, I had you in my mind, and you would always be there, in the back of my mind, so I...

Girl: Well, I'm here. I am back here.
I've been back for a little while.

Woman: Good, so I just wanted to say that you should, you know, cut the crap, and really live, you know, and stop fucking around. And that you shouldn't listen to anyone about how you should live, or what's true for you, but that you should get on with really living and look inside yourself, or whatever. Because even if you think you don't know, you know, what to do, you do, deep inside yourself, you do, you really do.

Girl: Ok. But why should I listen to you then? Because you just told me not to listen to anyone outside of myself, so why should I take this advice and listen to you?

Woman: Yes, right, OK, don't listen to me.
(This is the game they play...) That's right. Uh huh, um hum, ulh, right? Ulgh. Well that's it *(kind of 'fuck it')*...so long. Take it easy, but take it, ok?

(Gets up to go)

Girl: *(Quietly)* Are you drunk? I can't quite tell.

Woman: *(Pausing)* Yes. Oh yes I am...Are you?

Girl: No, actually. No, I'm not.

Woman: Are you drinking?

Girl: No, I'm not.

Woman: *(Pausing)* Well, good. Ok, good for you. So that's all. Ok. Oh. *(She starts to go.)*

Girl: Hey, you know, I really kind of owe you an apology, or whatever, because I really blamed you for something, for messing me up, and I know it wasn't you, it was me. I was just looking for someone to blame.

Woman: Oh, no, oh no, no, I was to blame. I am to blame.

Girl: No, really, I have to take responsibility for...

Woman: NO. That's adults. Adults have to take the responsibility. But children, children are not to blame, it's not their fault or responsibility. Things are done to children by adults. I came in here and did something to you. I spoke a, I broke a trust. I told you things that you were not prepared to hear, that you had not been prepared for, adult things, things that require preparation and experiences to understand and to cope with. I revealed secret things, secret adult things, and the consequences of that were that you had a knowledge you were not prepared for. And that is what wrecked you, and that is my fault.

Girl: Yeah, but you didn't really wreck me.
I mean, I'm not wrecked anymore.

Woman: I sincerely hope that is true.
Girl: It is. I mean, I'm kind of glad that it happened. That you came up here and I met you. Because I wouldn't know what I know now if you hadn't told me, if you hadn't hurt me and scared me, if I hadn't suffered, if I hadn't, you know...

Woman: I don't think that's right. What you're saying. I can't... I didn't expect you to be like this, when I came here, when I came back here.
But it doesn't change anything.

Girl: Well, I don't know what you expected, really, but as far as changing anything goes, I mean actually, it changes everything. That's what I think, in my deepest self, that everything can change, and even if it changes for the worse, it can change again, and keep changing.

Woman: *(Suddenly angry)* Look, I tried to be, I tried to come in here and speak with you in a real way, simply, but... you don't know. You can't know.

Girl: What can't I know? What's the big mystery? I know about feeling sick. About walking around sick in yourself and being dead but walking around, doing disgusting sick things that make you even sicker but not feeling anything anyway, just thumps on dull meat. I do know.

Woman: NO, kid. Uh uh. No, oh no. No. Everything is still ahead of you. There's still time for you to change or do whatever you fucking want to do. And that is why you can't know. You don't know what it's like when there is no time, when it's too late. It's just all used up. There's nothing left. It's like swimming down a river. At a certain point you really exhaust yourself, you just want to let the river take you, to let the current take you. That's what I'm doing, I'm just doing it with my mouth open.

Girl: So you really didn't change, when you came back here. You said you had, but you hadn't.

Woman: Yeah, that's right, I never could change. Not really.

Girl: Well, that's...

Woman: *(Interrupting)* Yes, that's.

Girl: Ok then, you'd better go.

Woman: Yes I had better.

Girl: I forgive you.

Woman: *(Startled, but tired of it now)* What?

Girl: I forgive you...

Woman: Ok great. *(Opening door to go out.)*

Girl: For what you're doing.

Woman: For what I did.

Girl: No, for what you're doing now.
I forgive you for what you're doing right now.

Woman: *(Sarcastic)* You forgive me?

Girl: Yes I do. In my deepest self.

Woman: *(Moved but unmoved)* Huh. Thanks. Thank you.

*(She goes out. The girl watches her,
then lies back down to go to sleep.)*

– The End –

Jenny Magnus & Guy Massey in *Round and Round*

Round and Round: a sexfarcetragedy

Premiered 2001
The Lunar Cabaret
Chicago, IL

Performed by Mark Comiskey, Jenny Magnus,
Guy Massey, & Colm O'Reilly
Directed with Beau O'Reilly

Round and Round: a sexfarcetragedy

CHARACTERS

The Woman:
Older, glamorous, elegant but faded, powerful but on the downside of the power, accustomed to getting what she wants and shocked when thwarted. Not a nice person masquerading as a bitch—actually a bitch. Believes everyone is as manipulative as she is (and, in fact, mostly, they are). Not a sentimentalist. Ultimately, intellectually honest.

The Old Friend:
Older, elegant, cultured, refined, terribly frustrated over years by arrangements that seem impossible to escape, amused by antics and preposterous posturing; somewhat above it all, but deeply caring and hurt, too. Could've been a humanitarian, if it had been socially acceptable.

The Young Friend:
In over his head much of the time, confused and frustrated at not being taken seriously, but a serious, devious person in his own right. Probably inwardly much less decent than the woman, just doesn't know it yet. Has yet to experience the depth of his own selfishness, and is shocked to find it so. The very definition of "callow."

The Honest Man:
A user, a leech; shameless and self-righteous; doesn't bother to lie. His honesty is not based in integrity: rather, he doesn't care enough about anyone else to soften anything. Thinks himself somewhat zen in his detachment, but really raging and entitled inside. He must have a moustache.

The Interlocutor:
Wry, detached, but human and invested.
Not a judging presence. Seeking to understand.

SETTING

The play is set on a huge lazy susan turntable that the actors turn during the action. The time is not specified, other than a post-apocalyptic Klimt-ish decayed wealth feeling, the turntable resembling, upon closer inspection, perhaps a rotting cake. The lazy susan is not required, perhaps only three rooms, each coming to focus when a scene plays in it.

The three rooms suggested are: a boudoir, with a daybed; a sitting room, with two upholstered chairs; and an ascetic's cell, with a hard bench and little else.

The style of play is stilted and formal, with sudden, violent departures. Transitions are set to music and sounds of creaking ships and groaning wood, with children's games like London Bridge played joylessly. The scenes move from one room to another, with all actors on stage all the time, neutral in the other rooms if the scene doesn't involve them, sometimes appearing to listen; at other times, not.

The disguises are absurdly small: a fake moustache, lipstick. The characters accept the disguises without trouble, until or unless they are unmasked.

The scenes with the Interlocutor are interrogations, with the interviewee stepping off the turntable and facing into a harsh light. The Interlocutor is unseen, a voice coming over a sound system.

The Woman and the Young Friend in Her Boudoir

Woman: What are you waiting for? Just say it.

Young: I don't want to just "say" it; I want to say it… well.

Woman: Why?

Young: Because I feel like whenever I just say it,
you jump on it and pick it apart.
I want to say it so it isn't vulnerable to you.

Woman: I think I've got to pick it apart, if it's full of holes.
It's my sworn duty, as a friend.

Young: Are we friends?

Woman: Yes, I think so.

Young: I don't.

Woman: No? Why not?

Young: Because you are so cruel to me at times.

Woman: Yes, but I am also so loving. Just the other day,
didn't I hold your balls in my hand and not squeeze?
I am so loving, I give you pleasure.

Young: Pleasure and loving are not the same thing.

Woman: You don't have to tell me that. I know very well what
vast differences there are between pleasure and love.

Young: You demonstrate them constantly.

Woman: Yes, well, I think it's my sworn duty as a friend to demonstrate them to you. What kind of friend would I be if you couldn't look to me for the purest expression of both pleasure and love?

Young: Who swore you to anything?

Woman: I did, of course, when I decided to become your friend.

Young: You are not my friend.

Woman: I am your greatest friend, only you'll never know it or admit it.

Young: In any case, I am now ready to say what I came here to say.

Woman: Please do.

Young: I want to ask you…
No, I want to tell you that I don't want you to <u>see</u> me anymore. That, even if I am around, which I will be, there's no doubt about that, it can't be helped, I want you to absent your attention from the situation when I am in it. I want us to remain as separate as possible and to have no contact anymore.

Woman: …Odd. But you don't expect either one of us to leave or go away from one another?

Young: Well, neither one of us can leave, you know that. I know I can't. And in fact, that is why I make this request of you, that <u>you</u> take the responsibility to stay distant from me, even if I can't from you, even if I speak to you, or beg you, or demand your attention.

Woman: How do I know if you're serious? How do I know this is your true desire? What if you do come to me tomorrow with equal, or even greater, well, "ardor," and beg for my attention? Am I supposed to assume that this today was what you wanted, and tomorrow you're only joking, or worse, testing me, or something, trying my resolve? An elaborate trap that you want to spring me into?

Young: I am serious. I offer you a challenge. If you can stay withdrawn from me, no matter what I do or say, I will give you something you have always wanted and never been able to get.

Woman: What could be within your power to give me?

Young: My absolute loyalty to you and to our, well, love.

Woman: I have always considered that already mine.

Young: I know, and you have been wrong.

Woman: But how can I be sure this is what you really want? How do I know this isn't just a very clever game that you've thought up on your way here today to play with me? I would hate to think you were thinking you were putting anything over on me.

Young: You don't know, you can't know, and that is the challenge to you. What are you capable of in the face of not knowing? To what lengths are you willing to go with no guarantees? It's a great compliment to you, actually, what I am asking.

Woman: Yes, right, I can see you think it is. But, obviously, I can't answer right away. I have to consider my response before I give it to you… I will say this, this is certainly the most serious, imaginative thing you have ever brought me to consider. I am really so amused by this leap forward in your sensibility. I've had an impact on you, I see.

Young: That's fair. I'll go away for now and come back later and we can finish this order of business.

Woman: Good, I am very pleased.

Young: I soon hope to be very pleased.

The Woman and the Old Friend in His Sitting Room

Woman: I've just been speaking to our friend. He made me the most remarkable challenge.

Old: What is it?

Woman: He wants me to have restraint in his presence.

Old: That doesn't seem very difficult to me.

Woman: Well, yes, but you're not affected by him in the way that I am. When I see him, smell him, hear his voice, I must say I am not interested in restraint.

Old: That's very funny, I always think of you as being primarily interested in restraint.

Woman: Only because what we share is heightened by it, my friend.

Old: Maybe so, but you've always been so contemptuous of the lack of restraint in other people. You have been particularly delighted in telling stories about people that center hilariously around their excesses.

Woman: Just because I find something amusing in someone else doesn't mean I mayn't have the same habit, or can't be interested in it. You know, the funniest thing about the whole idea is that he wants me to be the one to hold back. He doesn't expect any such thing from himself, in fact, if I know him, he'll try his utmost to undermine the whole arrangement.

Old: I don't know.

Woman: He wants me to pay no attention to him,
no matter how he begs or cries, and in exchange
for that, he'll give me his loyalty and love.

Old: But how will you know it?

Woman: Know what?

Old: Know that you have his love and not his contempt,
or indifference? It's possible he won't beg and
he'll just be gloating at your gullibility. He might
be relieved to be rid of you. He might even brag
about this little deal to all of his friends.

Woman: He doesn't have any friends other than me,
first of all, and secondly, I won't know, and
that's the really interesting thing about it. It's a
weird kind of faith, what he's asking from me,
the faith that he loves me even though
he wants me to leave him alone.

Old: Why does he want you to leave him alone?

Woman: I didn't ask him.

Old: I would have asked that the first thing.

Woman: Yes, well that is where we differ, my friend.
I think that his reasons for asking this of me
are less interesting than the possible
consequences of this experiment.

Old: Did you put a time limit on it?

Woman: No.

Round and Round: a sexfarcetragedy

Old: So this could a permanent condition, this "restraint"?

Woman: Yes, I suppose so. It doesn't really matter, though, because if I agree to try this, it's going to change my feelings towards him anyway.

Old: How can you say that? It seems to me like it would inflame you all the more.

Woman: No, I think the coal of the flame is the discourse <u>about</u> the flame. If we never speak, never even look at each other, how can we exchange meaningful remarks and secret glances? How can we intensify the friction? All our private jokes disappear, the eros flattens, and the energy between us dissipates.

Old: That's assuming you know where the origin of the energy is. You assume it's in the mind. What if it is originally in the body, as you say, the scent of him, the very sound of his voice may be what produces the energy, and you can't legitimately sequester yourself from that, not if you take the bet as it is. My understanding is that you will be still in the company of one another, right?

Woman: Yes, that's true.

Old: I think it's a bad bet. You shouldn't take it.

Woman: You have so little imagination.
Where you see me quivering with suppressed desire,
I see a whole universe of expansive possibilities
opening up.
What about the power and energy I'll get
from being quite good at restraint?
It's worked for us, my friend, it's worked for us.

Old: We never made a bet.

Woman: Well, this isn't technically a bet, it's a challenge.
So less is at stake.

Old: Is that what he says?
What if you don't agree to the challenge?

Woman: I don't know, we didn't discuss it.

Old: If I were you, I'd want to know what you give up
if you don't accept the challenge.

Woman: That's sensible of you, to want to know all the
details before agreeing to anything.

Old: Look what it's cost me to not have done that
in the past.

The Woman and the Young Friend in Her Boudoir

Woman: I have decided to accept the challenge under one condition.

Young: What's that?

Woman: I will agree to completely shut you out, and make no response to you at all, even if you speak to me or beg, I will do all that, only if you will agree to act with perfect abandon around me.

Young: What?

Woman: You heard me. I will only enter into this challenge with you if you will strip off the exterior façade of control and social acceptability, and become as close to being exactly as you truly are in the given moment, no matter how resistant you or anyone else is to whatever you find yourself doing.

Young: I don't know if I am capable of doing that.

Woman: Well, it certainly isn't fair to ask me to do something which I may be incapable of and then not be willing to risk something yourself.

Young: But I don't think I've ever acted with abandon at all, much less around you or anyone else.

Woman: Yes, you've always been a very…tactful person.

Young: By abandon do you mean deliberately trying to shock people?

Woman: I mean whatever it is you actually feel.
If you feel like shocking people, then you will.
If you feel like being blank and deadened, then you do that. Whatever is true to your deepest self.

Young: I'm not sure I know what is true to my deepest self.

Woman: Yes, well, therein lays the challenge, right?

Young: And if I agree to go all out and become completely, I don't know, myself, then you will agree to act as though I don't exist, no matter what I might do, to you or to myself?

Woman: Yes. Under that condition I will play your game.

Young: I have to think about this before I agree.

Woman: Oh yes, of course, I understand. You let me know.

The Young Friend and the Honest Man in His Cell

Young: I have to ask you a favor.

Honest: I have no time for your little business.
Leave me alone.

Young: No, I can't, I have to ask you something that only you can help me with.

Honest: Oh, for shit's sake, what is it? You're always so pathetic with your whining…Ah, whatever.

Young: I know you don't like me.

Honest: No, I don't like you.
I find you false and weak and polite.

Young: I know you think I am weak, and that is why I need to speak to you about something.
I am weak, I need help in order to get stronger.

Honest: Alright, what is it?

Young: I know you have a reputation for being, well, direct and blunt.

Honest: Again, a tremendously weak opening. Direct and blunt. You find me direct and blunt. Look, just say whatever you think you have to say and get on with it.

Young: I want you to instruct me in this…direct bluntness.

Honest: What? Impossible, forget it. So long.

Young: No, please, listen just for a moment.
I have a friend who has made me a terrible challenge.
I must separate myself from this friend, but I am
unable to be actually physically separate from her
because of our… circumstances. So I asked her,
as a friend, to separate herself from me in her
attentions, to shut me out, in my presence,
no matter how tortured it made me, and she said
she would, on one condition, only, if I agreed to
act in "perfect abandon" around her. So now I am
tortured all the more, because I don't know how to
do that, I don't even know what abandon is, yet I
must separate from her, and I know can't and I know
she can, she can do it. So I must act with abandon.
So, I want you to teach me how…to have abandon.

Honest: (*Thinking*)   This is actually interesting
to me in a frivolous kind of way.
Do you even know what abandon means?

Young: To lose yourself?

Honest: Yeah, that's it. So what is the difficulty?
Take a good look in the mirror and then, get lost

Young: So you think I have to see myself truly first,
see myself as I truly am, and then…

Honest: No, you first have to stop being so literal.
Or… become more literal. Ach, no, forget it,
I can't do anything for you, I think you should
just resign yourself to being tortured.

Young: How do you do it?

Honest: What?

Young: How do you act with abandon?

Honest: Who says I do?

Young: Well, your reputation…

Honest: You have to listen more to the evidence of your senses than to what other stupid fucking people say about anything. That's the first lesson. And be a tiny bit more critical in your thinking, if that's at all possible. Which I think it isn't. And above and beyond all of that, if I do agree to help you in some way in which I can't imagine, what do I get in return? Why should I do anything for you unless you do something for me?

Young: What can I do for you?
You really seem to have no use for me.

Honest: It's true, I find you a dope and an idiot, and I can hardly speak to you let alone…No…wait…

Young: What?

Honest: I just got a wonderful idea. There *is* something you can do for me. *(Pause)* If I agree to help you, oh christ, with learning how to be more, what, intrinsically <u>you</u>—jesus fucking christ how lame—then, you must agree to…impersonate me.

Young: Impersonate?
How in the world could I impersonate you?

Honest: I'll teach you how.

Young: But no one would ever accept me as you.

Honest: That's the second lesson, to open your mind and rid yourself of prejudice. You don't have any idea what people will accept or not accept. I think this is an excellent agreement.

Young: We haven't made an agreement, I haven't agreed to this exchange. I have to think about whether I can do what you're asking of me.

Honest: Take my word for it, you can. And you will. If you want me to show you how to open up to your true self, man.

Young: I can't answer right away. I have to think this over.

Honest: We'll get rid of that habit first off.

Round and Round: a sexfarcetragedy

The Interlocutor to the Woman

Interlocutor: Did you ever fuck him?

Woman: No. Or…

Interlocutor: Yes?

Woman: Maybe once. A long time ago.

Interlocutor: You don't remember?

Woman: It wasn't much.

Interlocutor: For him?

Woman: More.

Interlocutor: Ah.

Woman: Yes.

Interlocutor: Oh well. Never tried again?

Woman: Probably. I didn't notice.

Interlocutor: No wonder.

Woman: What?

Interlocutor: His hunger.

Woman: Yes. The appetite deferred…

Interlocutor: Is the appetite incurred.

Woman: Indeed.

The Woman and the Old Friend in His Sitting Room

Old: How is the little friend? Agreed to your proposal?

Woman: *(Distracted)* No, he hasn't answered yet.

Old: He seems to be taking his time.

Woman: Yes, he is slow.

Old: What's the matter? You seem distracted.

Woman: Do I? I don't…

Old: What are you planning? Whenever I see you in this state, it's inevitably because you have some wonderful revenge planned, or a terrible gift, someone is going to get a little something.

Woman: No, I don't think I have anything planned. On the contrary.

Old: You really seem disturbed. What's the matter?

Woman: I am disturbed. Ever since the last conversation I had with our young friend, I have had a very insistent thought in my mind. I can't get rid of it and it's bothering me very much, frankly.

Old: What is it?

Woman: I keep thinking that…oh, it's absurd, I can't bring myself to say it out loud.

Old: Even to me?

Woman: Even to you, though normally I take you so little seriously that I wouldn't care at all what you would think of this idea, but there it is: I am embarrassed by thinking this.

Old: Well, I never thought I'd see the day when you would be embarrassed.

Woman: I know, it's strange. I am completely unfamiliar with this feeling.

Old: Just tell me. I won't laugh.

Woman: I'll try to tell you, to describe it. After I told our young friend that I would accept his proposal of cutting him out if, and only if, he would become utterly un-self-conscious around me, I had a thought, after he left. What would it be like to watch him struggle to shrug off his façade, and how much amusement I would get from that, and then when I settled down to have a good laugh about it, I found that it didn't seem funny, it seemed, I felt sad, in some way, that I would have to be indifferent to that struggle, and that he would never know it if I felt that he was exciting, or terrible, or stupid, or dear, and I got really sad, and…

Old: You got sad?

Woman: Yes, isn't that strange, and I have been sad ever since, even though we haven't yet made our arrangement, the deal has not been struck, it's as though it had been, it may as well have been, because I feel vastly differently now. I would have been expecting something like frustration, or lust, or triumph, or even boredom, an emotion like that, but I feel absolutely, well, hurt about it instead.

Old: You feel hurt?! I am, I must admit, incredulous.

Woman: So am I. I didn't even know what it was at first, I thought it was something physically wrong with me, I felt this pain, right here, (*indicates heart*) and I even called the doctor, this is unbelievable, and I was fine physically, but the thought won't leave my mind that something has been lost, I've squandered something, and I will never be able to get it back.

Old: (*Pause*)   Oh I get it! This is part of your scheme, isn't it? You're enlisting me as an accomplice without my knowing it, because it will be all the more triumphant if you let the story get around that you have regrets, and it will get back to our little friend and then…

Woman: No, I wish it were that, but it isn't.
I feel very confused and not myself. In fact something feels torn inside of me, broken up, and everything I thought I knew and held up to be important and true about myself and about life, actually, seems to be crumbling in front of me.

Old: This is too overly dramatic.

Woman: Maybe, but I am telling you exactly what my experience is. I really feel lost.

Old: I have to say that this is the most ridiculous thing I ever heard in my life. A person doesn't just change into someone else because of an idea, because of a game.

Woman: Maybe not, but there it is. I don't know what to do.

Old: If I were you I would go away for a while and stop thinking these tedious thoughts.

Woman: I don't want to go away. I don't want to do anything.

Old: You need someone to take charge of you.
I will bring you away with me, if you let me.

Woman: You'll bring me…

Old: Yes, even though you may not believe it, I am capable of being dominating, with other people I am even known for being dominant; it's only with you I submit to your vision of the world. But in this case it's impossible, I can't submit to this, it alters everything way too much. You will just have to come with me when I leave. A change of scene will bring you right back to your old self.

Woman: I don't know if I can do that.

Old: I'll <u>make</u> you do it.

Woman: Let me think about it for a little while. Maybe you're right. But give me some time to consider it.

Old: All right, but I won't wait long.

The Woman and the Young Friend as the Honest Man in Her Boudoir

(The Young Friend enters in disguise as the Honest Man. His disguise, throughout, is as simple as a fake moustache.)

Woman:	What do you want?
Young as Honest:	I've come to thank you for your customary generosity with my customary appreciation.
Woman:	Oh, never mind about it—I'm in no mood for you today.
Young as Honest:	But I don't care to not mind. We have an arrangement and I am here to pay for my part of the bargain.
Woman:	Consider it a gift this time.
Young as Honest:	I am neither one who accepts nor gives gifts, Madam, you know this about me because you yourself pointed it out. Now let us get on with it; your reticence is charming, I'm sure, but I haven't got time for it.
Woman:	I'm telling you I don't need you, I don't want anything from you…
Young as Honest:	What you need is of no concern to me; my only concerns are my own needs, and I need to have no outstanding obligations. It doesn't suit my temperament. As you know. Which is why I entered into this arrangement to begin with.

> *(He forces her into a sexual position, perhaps he will be about to suck her off.)*

Woman: Leave me alone, stop touching me...

Young as Honest: Is this a new wrinkle, Madam?
You want me to act the beast?
Fine, then I will overpower you, as you like.
Let's get it over with.

Woman: No, stop it, stop...

> *(She really gets upset as he is sexual toward her, crying horribly but not really resisting.)*

Young as Honest: For shit's sake, what is the matter with you?

Woman: I don't want you.

Young as Honest: Well I don't want you either,
so what is the problem?

Woman: I want it to go back to how it was before.
I want it to be the way it was.

Young as Honest: It can never be the way it was,
it can only be the way it is.
Now let's get this over with.

> *(They struggle, the Woman knocks off the Young Friend's disguise and he is now revealed for himself.)*

Woman: What are you doing?
What does this mean? Is it you?

Young: (*Tightly wound*)
Yes, obviously it is, now please let us continue.

Woman: How could you deceive me in this way?
I thought you were Him.

Young: I know what you thought, but now that you know the truth, you must respect our arrangement. I am trying to do what you asked me to do, which is more than I can say for you in this moment.

Woman: But we never made the agreement,
we only spoke of it.

Young: As far as I am concerned, we made it, because I entered into other agreements based <u>upon</u> that arrangement. So if you please, stop this disturbance and let me carry out this task, so that I can continue to live up to our bargain.

Woman: No, I won't agree to this. I need…

Young: (*Losing it*)
This is goddamned fucking bullshit! I am so… Goddamn you. How can you crack at the first challenge? I overestimated you severely, obviously. You're absurdly weak, completely incapable of carrying out the simplest agreement.
This makes me rethink the entire bargain…

Woman: But we never even struck the bargain, we never agreed to anything, it was all still in negotiation. Please, let's stop this fighting and talk about it calmly. I feel differently than I did, I want to make a different arrangement…

Young: Just shut your mouth and don't say any more.
Stop talking to me. Don't look at me.
I am so disgusted with you, I can't even think.
I trusted you! You're selfish and more stupid and
cruel than I ever even thought.

Woman: Please reconsider.

Young: I have to get away and think this over.

Woman: Let's try something else.

Young: I can't think straight with you here. Fucking bitch.

Woman: *(Shocked)* I am begging you.

The Interlocutor to the Old Friend

Interlocutor: Did you ever fuck her?

Old: Yes.

Interlocutor: And…?

Old: It wasn't much.

Interlocutor: Oh. So…

Old: But I never told her.

Interlocutor: No?

Old: Why burst her bubble?

Interlocutor: I see.

Old: She didn't seem to like it either.

Interlocutor: So why not be honest?

Old: She liked to think me panting.

Interlocutor: So you…

Old: I gave that to her. It's not much really. If you think about it.

Interlocutor: Not much…?

Old: To give someone that power. She enjoyed it.

Interlocutor: And you?

Old: It gave me power. To give her power.

The Old Friend and the Honest Man in His Cell

Honest: Well, you haven't been here in a long while, my old friend. I haven't missed you, but now that you're here, I am glad.

Old: (*Almost gleeful*)
I have something very important to discuss with you.

Honest: Something important? It must be a development, otherwise I wouldn't see you.

Old: Yes, it's a development. Indeed, a wonderful development, and a satisfying one as well. You have, at long last, lost. You have lost and I have won.

Honest: I have lost? In what sense do you mean?

Old: You know very well what I mean. She is coming away with me, and so you have lost your wager with me.

Honest: She is coming away with you?

Old: Yes, well, she has agreed to think it over. In any case, I feel confident that she will at last be with me, and from there it is only a matter of time before she turns toward me.

Honest: You must be confident, to come here on the strength of her agreement to think it over.

Old: Yes, well, you should have seen her, she was unlike I've ever seen her before, quite vulnerable actually, and weak. Had I not been so triumphant and pleased I would have been shocked.

Honest: Weak, you say? It's too bad I haven't been to see her then, I would probably find that amusing.

Old: You haven't seen her?
But isn't this your day to go and see her?

Honest: Yes, in fact it is, but I have made another arrangement, thank god, because it has been increasingly intolerable for me to see her.

Old: What other arrangement?

Honest: I organized a trade with our young friend, concerning lessons in self and abandon thereof.

Old: You organized a trade?
What did you get for your lessons?

Honest: He agreed to impersonate me in situations where I no longer felt inclined to be but didn't want to lose the benefits of. And my visits with her are most certainly one of those situations.

Old: So our young friend went to see her, what, as you?

Honest: Yes, and I have to admit he took to it better than I thought he would. My instinct told me he didn't have it in him to be like me, but I was quite wrong.

Old: You sent our young friend to see her, when she is in this state, and he went as you?

Honest: Yes, we've established that. I can see that you are bothered by the idea of this. Why might that be? Hmmm, maybe it's because your little gloating fit just now is suddenly shakier than you thought. Perhaps congratulations are not quite in order, my capitulation not as assured?

Old: You are so unbelievable. No matter what I do, over all these years, somehow you always win.

Honest: I don't think we can leap to that conclusion, but I agree that I often win, and in this particular bet, I believe beyond a shadow of a doubt, I will win. She is never going to turn to you, will never need you, no matter what happens.

Old: How can you be so sure?

Honest: Because she really just doesn't care at all. Bottom line. She just doesn't…care.

Old: If you'd have seen her, though, she was so different.

Honest: No, you and she just thought for the moment that she was different.

Old: You think you know everything.

Honest: No, I only think I know her.

Old: I think you're wrong.

Honest: Want to bet?

Old: I have to go and see her again, first.

Honest: A weak parlay, but I'll agree to it, only because I also know you, and that you'll come back and bet me, and continue to lose for as long as I am interested in betting with you, which probably isn't much longer.

The Honest Man and the Woman in Her Boudoir

Woman: I don't want to see you, leave me alone.

Honest: I won't leave you alone, I'm furious, you've broken our agreement, and I wanted to see the truth of the situation for myself.

Woman: Alright, you see the truth. Here I am, just me, as I am, and I am crippled in some terrible way by this young friend, and I am incapable of disguising it or…

Honest: (*Yelling*)   You agreed! You agreed to let me be the one! All this time I went along and showed you nothing but contempt, and went against everything I felt, and I did it because of our agreement, and now you are trying to change it, and I won't allow it! Do you hear me!? I won't allow it.

Woman: Alright, yes, I broke our agreement, not because I wanted to, it just happened. I couldn't help it.

Honest: That is complete bullshit. Nothing just happens, one creates it, you yourself told me that and I believed you and knew you were right. You can't tell me that this enormous effort on my part to conceal myself from you, and everyone else, was for nothing! After all this time, it wasn't for nothing!

Woman: I'm so ashamed.

Honest: You disgust me. How could I have ever agreed to this and kept it up all this time, if I had an inkling of the mediocrity you are displaying now—I would never have even spoken to you. I thought you were a worthy adversary. You're pathetic.

Woman: Alright, all right, enough. Stop abusing me.
I know how you feel.

Honest: That is the entire point of my rage, Madam:
that you suddenly know or care how I feel.
This changes everything.

Woman: *(Desperate)* It doesn't change everything.
I…don't want to change everything.

Honest: It's too late, and anyway, what you want no longer
interests me.

Woman: I'm sorry, I'm so sorry, please, please,
I need your help.

Honest: What? Are you kidding?

Woman: No, as you were talking, I suddenly realized you were
the only one who could help me. Please help me.

Honest: I have no fucking inten—

Woman: Listen, I need you to create a diversion, yes, to make
a diversion behind which I can recover myself. I feel
so exposed, and I can't think straight with everyone
or anyone seeing me this way.

Honest: A diversion? What the fuck does that mean?

Woman: I need you to pretend you've had a change of heart
towards me.

Honest: I have had one; just listen to what I am saying.

Woman: No, I need you to pretend to take pity on me.

Honest: Take pity?! Impossible, no one will believe it.

Woman: I know why you say that, but I think that if you played it just right, it would be absurd enough to be above suspicion. You're right, no one would believe it and that's why it would work.

Honest: I don't know. I have to think about it.
My reputation is at stake.

Woman: Please think about it, I don't know what else to try.

The Interlocutor to the Young Friend

Interlocutor: Did she ever fuck you?

Young: Many times.

Interlocutor: And?

Young: Good. It got better, actually.

Interlocutor: Oh, that's nice.

Young: Yes, it was nice.

Interlocutor: Better for her too?

Young: I don't know. We never discussed it.

Interlocutor: Why not?

Young: Didn't want to break the spell. Draw attention to it.

Interlocutor: I see.

Young: Do you?

Interlocutor: No.

Young: Ever had a great dream, and then, in the telling, it sounded like nothing?

Interlocutor: Yes, of course.

Young: It's rather like that.

The Young Friend as the Honest Man and the Old Friend in His Sitting Room

Old: What do you want? Here to gloat?

Young as Honest: No, I want to tell you that I have been to see her and I am prepared to quit our bet.

Old: What?!

Young as Honest: Yes, I am prepared to quit the whole messy business. I want no more part of it, it doesn't amuse me anymore, I give it over to you and you can have the whole thing.

Old: Has everyone gone insane? What are you talking about? How can you quit our bet? It doesn't make any sense.

Young as Honest: It does make sense, it makes nothing but sense. She's clearly disturbed, and I have no interest in gaining anything through that disturbance. I no <u>longer</u> have any interest.

Old: What did she say to you that would make you change your mind so radically?

Young as Honest: She asked me to take pity on her.

Old: Pity?! That is unthinkable.

Young as Honest: Yes, and strangely enough, I do.

Old: You take pity on her. Well now I've heard everything. First, I never imagined you were capable of pity, and secondly, that you would even entertain the idea of taking it on her, on someone who has tortured you for years, forcing you to service her in the most humiliating manner, with no thought to your feelings. I can't believe it.

Young as Honest: Whether you believe it or not, it is true, and in fact I am glad. Glad to be rid of our bet, which has bored me for years, and glad to be rid of her, who has not, but soon will, I am sure. She is changed, utterly changed, and so miserable and pathetic that it ceases to be fun to despise her. So there it is, take it or don't, it doesn't matter to me. Though it does mean now that I will need support and donation from somewhere else, and I would be a fool to not expect it from you, as you essentially owe me from losing our bet.

Old: Losing! I thought you capitulated!

Young as Honest: I only quit, I never said I lost.

Old: Well, it seems to me that if you quit, then that means you forfeit. Which means I win.

Young as Honest: Only if one has to follow some kind of rules about these things.

Old: Which you never do, of course.

Young as Honest: Of course not.

Old:	Well, obviously, I <u>can</u> support you, but why should I? You had an exchange with her for so many years, and she got something from you for that support, so what do I get?
Young as Honest:	Yes, it is difficult, certainly, as I am sure I have very little you might want. (*Pause*) Except, perhaps, my absolute loyalty to our, well, love.
Old:	Our love.
Young as Honest:	Yes.
Old:	I was unaware that we had any. Love.
Young as Honest:	Regardless of your awareness of it, we do.
Old:	Have we always?
Young as Honest:	Why yes.
Old:	Why haven't I known about it?
Young as Honest:	That is a question I wouldn't answer if I could.
Old:	I suppose not…It never ceases to amaze me that you…In fact, you never cease to amaze me.
Young as Honest:	And that is why you will support me.
Old:	(*Caught*) I…I…Oh, shit.

The Young Friend and the Honest Man in His Cell

Honest: Did you see him?

Young: Yes. In fact I did.

Honest: And?

Young: It went well, I think.

Honest: Good, tell me, details please, do I count on him for support or do I not?

Young: Yeeesss, I think you can.

Honest: That was a somewhat equivocal yes, I trust your explanation will clarify it.

Young: Well, I had to make an agreement with him…

Honest: An agreement. This should be good.

Young: Well, you can't have thought he was going to support you for nothing.

Honest: I can and did.

Young: Why should you think that people would give you money for no reason other than that you need it?

Honest: That is exactly the reason you idiot.

Young: If there is an idiot here, it seems to be you, if you really believe what you just said.

Honest: Idiot though I may be, I do expect to be supported, and in style, by my more well-cushioned friends. But be that as it may, get to the point. What do I have to do to get it from him?

Young: You must…love…him.

Honest: Love him?

Young: Yes.

Honest: As in fuck him?

Young: That wasn't specified.

Honest: Hm. Anything else?

Young: Yes, you must have loyalty to that love.

Honest: Oh, there's the rub. Loyalty. I must say, that may be beyond me.

Young: Love is not beyond you but loyalty is?

Honest: I suspect so.

Young: You are absurd. Loyalty is easy.

Honest: For you, perhaps.

Young: For anyone. There is no doubt in my mind that you can, at least, give the impression of loyalty. Enough of an impression to convince your old friend at any rate. He isn't the sharpest of fellows.

Honest: He's sharper than you think, and probably than you will ever be, though you will never know it.

Young: That's your first act of loyalty right there.
Now do you want me to continue, or…

Honest: No, I think you've done enough. You've done far better than I ever thought you could, but I don't need you anymore.

Young: I didn't know you needed me in the first place.

Honest: Slip of the tongue. By the way, have you seen her?

Young: Yes.

Honest: And?

Young: She's recovering, just as she thought she might, behind the cover of your professed pity. Though I am sure she will never be the same. Everyone is talking about how you protected her, and refused to denounce her. How anyone ever believed it is quite beyond me.

Honest: People will believe almost anything you tell them to believe, if you have the reputation for being honest.

Young: Which is utterly undeserved, I must say. It seems to me you are thoroughly insincere, and chronically inauthentic.

Honest: I see we have both benefited from our exchange.

The Interlocutor to the Woman

Interlocutor: Ever fuck him?

Woman: A lot.

Interlocutor: Any good?

Woman: Sometimes.

Interlocutor: Why sometimes?

Woman: Who knows?

The Woman and the Old Friend in Her Boudoir

Old: What are you waiting for? Just say it.

Woman: I don't want to just say it. I want to say it…well.

Old: Well or badly, I know what you are going to say, so do us both the favor of getting it over with.

Woman: You know he's taking advantage of you.

Old: Yes, of course I do, don't be so obvious.

Woman: Well, everyone is laughing at you.
You know that don't you?

Old: Of course, why should they do otherwise?
But they don't know everything about it, and so they are laughing out of ignorance.

Woman: Well, why are you supporting him?
What are you getting out of it?

Old: What do you think I am getting out of it?

Woman: I can't imagine. It couldn't be what I was getting.
I assume that would be of no interest to you.

Old: Perhaps your assumptions must be questioned, Madam; you certainly don't know everything about me.

Woman: I know enough.

Old: That is precisely the attitude which prevents you from knowing more.

Woman: In any case, it doesn't flatter you, I don't like you being in this position.

Old: It could never occur to you that I may be satisfied with the arrangement for reasons of my own?

Woman: No, because you would have told me the reasons if you were satisfied with them.

Old: In the past, perhaps. But at this point, it pleases me to keep the reasons to myself. Now, enough on this subject. Let me say you are seeming well.

Woman: Thank you, I am quite well again at last. I thought that spell would never be broken, but it is, and I am the better for it.

Old: Better in what way?

Woman: In that I have experienced a more…urgent conception of myself, I suppose, and in that way have been freed from the terrible restrictions I was laboring under.

Old: Which restrictions might those be?

Woman: All the arrangements and wagers and impossible agreements, I couldn't keep it straight anymore, I came to feel that all the false good was worse than actual evil, and I have shrugged it all off, and I feel that my intention is now wholly to myself, instead of to others.

Old: I have experienced your intention as always being wholly to yourself, my dear.

Woman: Yes, but in a way, all this time, I have been performing a service to all of you.

Old: A service? It seems to me that we have all been, quite literally, servicing you.

Woman: On the surface, yes, but the inner truth has been that my actions have been a continuous catalyst for all of you, and I have been a connecting force, a certain kind of contagion…

Old: A contagion?

Woman: Yes, I have thought long and hard about what my role has been. I have been providing the…

Old: The infection?

Woman: If you want to call it that. Regardless, I have been providing it, and now I can see clearly, the time has come for me to pull in my connections and try to become more…free floating.

Old: I doubt if you are capable of it my dear. It's not sour grapes which leads me to say it, even though you may think it is. I am, I must tell you, I am… disappointed that you have made no mention of coming away with me.

Woman: But that is unnecessary now, don't you see? I have recovered. I have recovered myself.

Old: And in the process you are willing to lose me?

Woman: Why must I lose you?

Old: If you have no need for me anymore, how can we expect to maintain any hold over each other?
I, too, become free floating.

Woman: You have never had a hold over me,
my dear. Don't flatter yourself.
It makes you quite unattractive.

Old: That remark goes to the essence
of my hold over you.

The Honest Man as the Old Friend and the Woman in Her Boudoir

Woman: Are you here again? I thought we had left it in a rather perfect balance between us. A tie.

Honest as Old: I didn't.

Woman: Oh really? You seemed fine when you left. It was only a short while ago…Did you forget to say something?

Honest as Old: No, not quite forgot…Or, yes, perhaps I did, yes, I forgot to say something. Something that has needed saying for quite some time.

Woman: Well, go ahead, then, say it.

Honest as Old: Yes, I will say it. I…I am in love with you and have always been, and it is a torture to me to be by your side in this way and never be able to acknowledge my feelings to you.

Woman: What in the world are you talking about?! You embarrass me. This is unlike you, to be so utterly bald. I don't want to hear you like this, after what we were just talking about, I…

Honest as Old: I don't care what we have just been talking about, Madam, I only care about what I am saying right now. You have treated me badly for years and I am no longer willing to accept that treatment.

Woman: You agreed to be treated that way. It isn't as though I ever forced anything upon you. We were both playing under clearly defined rules…

Honest as Old: I never defined them, you did. I merely acquiesced to them. They solidified around me. But now they no longer interest me.

Woman: I don't care if they ever interested you or not. In truth, these "rules" have been all we have ever shared, and so now if you want to discard them, you force me to…

Honest as Old: Listen to me, you will listen to me.

(*Something violent between them is going to happen.*)

Woman: (*Suddenly, dawning*)
Have you been talking to our friend?

Honest as Old: What? What do you mean?

Woman: Our friend. Our honest friend. Have you been spending time with him? Because I sense his hand in this tactic.

Honest as Old: This is not a tactic, my dear, in fact it is the first thing we have discussed that was not a tactic since we first met.

Round and Round: a sexfarcetragedy

Woman: Well, it seems like a tactic to me. Just when I find a way to declare my independence from you and all of your hovering, unrelentingly helpful presence, you, at that particular moment, decide to declare undying love and demand yet another form of dependence from me.

Honest as Old: Dependence is not what I wish from you.

Woman: All right, what do you exactly wish from me? As long as we are being so direct and honest, what is it you would have me do? Exactly?

Honest as Old: I would have you love me back, I suppose.

Woman: Alright. I do love you. I love you. (*Violently*) There it is.

Honest as Old: (*Pause*) Alright. Good. I am glad. Now if we can…

Woman: No, we can't. We can't do anything with that exchange. That exchange is over. That is not something I am willing to negotiate or organize, or in any way discuss.

Honest as Old: Then you create a rather impossible situation between us.

Woman: No, you have created the impossibility.
I am merely playing along with it, in my way.
These are _my_ moves, _my_ calculation.
Not, perhaps, what you may have been expecting or wishing for, but we play differently.

Honest as Old: (*Really angry*)
Madam, I am no longer playing!
Can't you get that in your mind?
I have stopped playing, and now
I only want resolution.

Woman: The resolution is that I win. The resolution is that things are as I say they are.
Take it or leave it.

Honest as Old: We shall see.

The Interlocutor to the Honest Man

Interlocutor: Ever fuck him?

Honest: God, no.

Interlocutor: Why not?

Honest: No, no.

Interlocutor: Why?

Honest: Are you blind? He's an idiot.

Interlocutor: So?

Honest: Idiots can't fuck well.

Interlocutor: Really?

Honest: Of course. No sense of humor.

Interlocutor: Well, maybe.

Honest: No, it's true. Self-seriousness is anti-erotic.

Interlocutor: To you, maybe.

Honest: We're talking about me.

Interlocutor: Actually, we're talking about him.
I don't find him idiotic.

Honest: You fuck him then, and let me know.

The Old Friend and the Honest Man in His Cell

Honest: I have been awaiting your presence, old friend, rather urgently.

Old: Why? (*Irksome*.) You knew I would be coming. There was never a doubt in your mind.

Honest: No doubt, you are right in that—rather, anticipation. We have necessary business to set into motion.

Old: Yes, yes, here I am, ready to support you in your inexplicable existence. Fine, you win.
I am at your service.

Honest: You seem somewhat peckish.
Somewhat more than usual. What's the matter?

Old: As if you cared. Let's just get on with it, shall we?

Honest: No, indeed, I see disturbance. The least I can do for your generosity is to be your confidante.
What is upsetting you?

Old: Oh, you just have to know, don't you?
So you can laugh and feel superior to your poor pathetic friend.

Honest: You misjudge me sir. I am, if nothing else, a loyal conspirator in one shared torment.

Old: Well, she has turned against me. Now you know.
She has somehow decided that I am below notice.

Round and Round: a sexfarcetragedy

Honest: How did this happen?

Old: It was when I went to see her, as usual, yesterday. We were speaking calmly of the change in her, her strange change of heart towards her former entanglements, and how it would, of course, affect me, and I left her somewhat less than pleasantly, but no more so than usual. And when I went to see her today, she actually would not agree to see me. She sent word that I was no longer welcome. Can you believe that? Never, in all the years of our acquaintance, has she refused me her company. I have just come from there.

Honest: She wouldn't see you. Today, or…?

Old: At all! I was disinvited. Very clearly.

Honest: What exactly was said?

Old: She sent a note! Here it is: "Since you have felt the need to speak to me in a way I cannot accept, I cannot see you anymore. Even if you are around, physically, which you will be, it can't be helped, there's no doubt about that, I will absent my attention from you, from the situation, if you are in it. We will remain as separate as possible and have no contact anymore. Please respect my wishes and do not beg, or speak to me, or demand my attention."

Honest: That sounds just like the deal she struck with our young friend.

Old: Yes, but that was a game to her.

Honest: Only at first. Then it turned into something else.

Old: Yes, but this is totally different, this just seems like she wants me to go away from her.

Honest: What did you say to her?

Old: Only that I didn't like this change in her.
That I thought it would change things between us.

Honest: Which it has.

Old: But not this drastically. When I think of all the years I have shown up only to be treated badly by her, and yet I have kept up my end. And now…

Honest: You'll be cut.

Old: Yes! This is infuriating.

Honest: Oh, be quiet. You're only getting what you deserve anyway. Pathetically hanging on for so long, secretly pining, imagining she would someday wake up and see you for who you really are. Well, she has, at last, seen you, and she rejects you. So get over it and redirect your attention to someone who deserves it.

Old: Like you, I suppose.

Honest: Of course.

The Young Friend and the Woman in Her Boudoir

Woman: Why are you here?

Young: I have been to see your old friend.

Woman: Yes?

Young: He is suffering.

Woman: Alright.

Young: Why are you hurting him?

Woman: It is for his own good. Why should you care?

Young: It seems unnecessary…You feel nothing towards him?

Woman: It is none of your concern.

Young: It is.

Woman: Why?

Young: I feel that this…

Woman: (*Interruptus*)   Oh, you feel. You feel so many things. Good. Good for you. Go away and feel them elsewhere.

Young: You don't want me here? I thought you wanted me to reconsider our arrangement? You said you wanted a different agreement, and…

Woman: I did. Now, I no longer care.

Young: Why not?

Woman: Because this whole business comes from your proposal to me. And now I have lost the dearest friend I ever had. Over someone as unimportant as you.

Young: You're sorry to lose his company?

Woman: Of course. You idiot. He is my oldest friend. I feel nothing but sorry.

Young: Then why?

Woman: Because he is in love with me and I am not with him. He came right out and said this to me, after all these years of unspoken understanding between us. So, once he has made it plain, I cannot allow him to go on making himself…small. He must be free of me whether he wants to or not. That, at least, is my sworn duty to him, as a friend.

Young: Yet you suffer…

Woman: Of course. How could it be otherwise? It is my loss. I must bear it.

Young: May I help you bear it?

Woman: Why would you want to do that?

Young: Because…I can.

Woman: Of course. Yet I no longer want you.

Young: That is exactly why I can help you.

The Interlocutor to the Young Friend

Interlocutor: Ever fuck her?

Young: Oh, no.

Interlocutor: Why not?

Young: Too scary.

Interlocutor: Scary? Like…

Young: She scares me.

Interlocutor: Too powerful?

Young: No, too mean. Too selfish.

Interlocutor: Like what?

Young: Like I would have to be sure she was happy all the time. Or she would be mean to me about it.

Interlocutor: You think so?

Young: Don't you?

Interlocutor: Well, okay, I can see it.

Young: I think it's obvious.

Interlocutor: So what if she were mean? Couldn't you be mean back?

Young: I suppose so, but would that be fun?

Interlocutor: Could be.

Young: Maybe.

Interlocutor: Why not try it? For the sake of experience?

Young: There are some experiences I don't want to have.

The Woman and the Honest Man in Her Boudoir

Woman: Our young friend has been to see me.

Honest: I know.

Woman: How do you know?

Honest: I suggested it.

Woman: Why?

Honest: Because I knew you no longer cared for him.

Woman: Ah…Perfect.

Honest: Yes, and now, you are free, really, to turn your attention to something far more important.

Woman: Which is what?

Honest: My welfare and satisfaction. I did what you asked, I risked my reputation and took pity on you, and I now want what is coming to me in return.

Woman: Do you really mean to tell me you want to return to our old arrangement? How tedious.

Honest: I agree. That would be tedious. That is not what I want. What I want is something entirely new. I want your absolute loyalty to our…well…love.

Woman: Our love! I was unaware that we had any. Love.

Honest: No you were not. But that doesn't matter. We do, and now I want it.

Woman: I don't know if I can do that.

Round and Round: a sexfarcetragedy

Honest: You can, and will.

Woman: Why will I? How will you make me?

Honest: I can offer you something you want.

Woman: What do you think I want?

Honest: It involves our old friend.

Woman: There is nothing you can do about that situation.

Honest: Oh yes there is. I can fix it so that he is no longer… small…with regards to you.

Woman: And how do you imagine you can do that?

Honest: I can. That is all you need to know.
Now are you interested or not?

Woman: I have to think it over.

The Honest Man and the Young Friend in His Cell

Honest: I want you to pay a visit to our old friend.

Young: Why?

Honest: That is far less interesting and important than you can possibly imagine.

Young: You have no idea what I can imagine.

Honest: (*Really looking at him for the first time*)
I think, in this one instance, you may be right. In any case, you will be well able to organize this for me.

Young: Organize it for you, <u>as</u> you?

Honest: (*Very sly*)
Of course. How otherwise?

The Young Friend as the Woman and the Old Friend in His Sitting Room

Old: I am surprised to see you.

Young as Woman: I know.

Old: What do you…want?

Young as Woman: To tell you something.

Old: I thought you were no longer speaking to me.

Young as Woman: I'm not. (*Private joke*)

Old: What? Oh what is it you want, tell me please.

Young as Woman: I want you to do me one last favor. I want you to…forgive me.

Old: What are you talking about?

Young as Woman: I think you know.

Old: "Forgive" you? For what?

Young as Woman: For having been selfish and unkind to you. For having treated you badly and for having made you small. I have become quite aware of the dishonorable way I have behaved towards you, and I am really quite…sorry…for it.

Old: (*Somewhat speechless*)   Are you serious?

Young as Woman:	Yes.
Old:	Well, alright, then, yes, I will consider your request.
Young as Woman:	Thank you for your kindness.
Old:	Are you, alright?
Young as Woman:	Yes.

The Woman and the Young Friend in Her Boudoir

Young: I have been to see our old friend.

Woman: We are no longer friends.

Young: He is your greatest friend.
Only you will no longer admit it.

Woman: In any case, I don't wish to discuss him.

Young: Oh, but it is my sworn duty, as a friend, to discuss him.

Woman: Who swore you to anything?

Young: I did, when I decided to become your friend.

Woman: Are we friends?

Young: Yes, I think so.

Woman: I don't.

Young: Why not?

Woman: Because you insist on bringing up this subject.

Young: It is my sworn duty…

Woman: (*Interruptus*) Enough.

Young: He has renounced you.

Woman: What?!

Young: You heard me.

Woman: Who asked you to see him? Or speak with him?

Young: No one. Yet I did it all the same.
For my own amusement.

Woman: I don't care if he renounces me or not.
What did he say?

Young: He said you had lost your charm.

Woman: He said that?

Young: Yes, and he said it was a relief to be free of you. He said he'd been awakened to your cruelty and banality. He said he found you tiresome. You had become all too human, and so lost your sheen.

Woman: Of course he would say all of that.
He has been spurned.

Young: He said you would say something like that.

The Interlocutor to the Woman

Interlocutor: Ever fuck him?
Woman: Yes.
Interlocutor: And…?
Woman: It didn't work out.
Interlocutor: But was it any good?
Woman: …It didn't work out.

The Woman as the Honest Man and the Young Friend in His Cell

Woman as Honest: What took you so long, you little devil? You know better than to keep me fucking waiting.

Young: Yes, yes, all of your games and machinations take up my time, and frankly I am becoming tired of them.

Woman as Honest: Well, soon all the machinations will be finished, I assure you.

Young: Good. What do you want? Why have you asked me to see you here?

Woman as Honest: I simply wished to be discreet, for once. I am interested in your interpretation of the situation. As it now stands.

Young: My interpretation of the situation?

Woman as Honest: Yes. In your opinion, how will all this end? Who will prevail? In addition to me, of course.

Young: You are interested in my opinion? I must admit, I am surprised.

Woman as Honest: Why? You have been an excellent student, after all, and the master always wants to see the fruit of his labor harvested. So demonstrate your newly acquired skills of analysis and provide me with the benefit of your insight. If you please.

Round and Round: a sexfarcetragedy

Young: Actually, I do please. This has all been most amusing. In fact, it occurred to me that in being challenged to act with abandon, I have been quite surprised by the qualities that have emerged when left utterly unchecked. A tremendous urge towards exploitation and deceit have been loosed, I quite enjoy it.

Woman as Honest: Evidently.

Young: Yes, and I also think that our mutual friends have been denuded of whatever prestige they once thought they had, and that they are now simply ripe for further manipulation to whatever ends I…or, of course, we, have impulses towards.

Woman as Honest: You believe them to be diminished?

Young: Utterly. In fact, at this point, they resemble each other. And they are beginning to know it.

Woman as Honest: Ah. So you find them both…

Young: Small. Both terribly small.
And growing smaller.

Woman as Honest: In what way?

Young: Oh, they begin to care for each other. And not in the sense of what they can get, as it has been up to now. No, no, they want the other to be alright, to not suffer. It's all so human and tender.

Woman as Honest: You find that small?

Young: Don't you?

Woman as Honest: No, on the contrary. I find it big of one to care for the other. Enough to make sacrifices for them, or even to lose them.

Young: *(Pause)* I think that is unlike you. To find it so.

(*Really looking at her as him, and continuing, carefully*)

But of course, you are always… unpredictable.

The Woman and the Young Friend in Her Boudoir

Woman: Come in.

Young: I only have one thing to say, Madam.

Woman: I know. I know.

Young: You know what I have to say.

Woman: Yes.

Young: Oh. Well, how do you respond?

Woman: I don't.

Young: Not at all?

Woman: No.

Young: Oh. Alright. Well.

Woman: Yes.

Young: And you?

Woman: Oh, nothing, nothing from me. Not today.

Young: Oh.

(They sit quietly together.)

The Interlocutor to the Old Friend

Interlocutor: Ever fuck her?

Old: Yes.

Interlocutor: And…

Old: It didn't work out.

Interlocutor: But was it any good?

Old: …It didn't work out.

The Old Friend and the Honest Man in His Sitting Room

Honest: I heard our friends have become reconciled.

Old: Have you?

Honest: Yes. As have you.

Old: Yes. Well.

Honest: And...

Old: What?

Honest: Your opinion?

Old: Oddly, I have none.

Honest: You have no opinion?

Old: No, I genuinely don't. I just don't...care.

Honest: It affects you.

Old: Perhaps.

Honest: It does.

Old: Alright.

Honest: And you counter with absolutely nothing?

Old: Nothing.

(They sit quietly together, laughing.)

The Young Friend and the Honest Man in His Cell

Honest: I have no time for your little business.
             Leave me alone.

Young: I feel as if the world is shrinking.
             I am watching everything recede,
             as I grow and grow it all gets farther
             and farther away. Smaller and smaller,
             soon it will certainly all disappear and
             I will be left with a spectacular view of nothing.

Honest: Probably. Our little circle, it bites its own tail.
             But so what?

Young: I don't know. What shall I do?

Honest: You could cut yourself. Off.

The Interlocutor to the Young Friend

Interlocutor: Ever fuck him?

Young: Yes.

Interlocutor: And…

Young: It didn't work out.

Interlocutor: But was it any good?

Young: …It didn't work out.

The Old Friend and the Woman in His Sitting Room

Old: I have been waiting for you.
Oh, I missed you so much.

Woman: I know, yes, oh yes.
I have been missing you terribly.

Old: Can we, at last, please…

Woman: No, stop. Let me speak.

Old: Alright.

Woman: Thank you. You are, as always, impeccably generous with me. I must tell you what has happened. I have lost, at long last I have lost, and you have won, and I am not sorry. There was a time when I would rather have died than hear myself say those things, but everything has changed, and resist it though I might, I have changed. I once asked you to give me something. Do you remember what it was?

Old: Yes, of course. My absolute loyalty to our love.

Woman: And you did. You unfailingly did.
Though I then asked you for another…

Old: A sacrifice, it was.

Woman: Yes, to be my confidant in the campaign I would wage against love. To stop loving you or anyone. I despised it and myself when I loved, found it agony to do so, I could not bear it. And so I stopped it. Wonderfully well. Any habit can be changed. And then, recently, I thought I loved again. Our young friend, a mistake in my thinking, I thought it was love

Round and Round: a sexfarcetragedy

>   but it wasn't, it was loss. I felt loss in relation to him.
>   And I don't know why, but the loss spiraled down,
>   round and round, and finally reached my friendship
>   with you. And I came to see that I simply couldn't live
>   in a world without you in it. Is that love? I don't know.
>   So I am here, to ask you, to ask if we can, can we…

Old: Why yes, my dear…Of course we can.
           My dear friend. You haven't lost, let's just quit,
           shall we? You owe me nothing. You owe me nothing.
           Let us simply go on together in this new way.
           I don't care about any of it anymore.

Woman: And yet, can you set aside your love for me?

Old: (*Very sadly*)
           No. I can't. But I can bring it with me. As we go.

Woman: What if I don't, or can't…

Old: I know you would, if you could.

Woman: Yes. Yes, that's it. I would. If I could.

The Woman and the Honest Man in Her Boudoir

Woman: I have asked you here to give you something.

Honest: I hope you are giving me what I have asked you to give.

Woman: I don't love you. I am sorry to have any feelings for you at all, probably. But I do, and so what I offer is a mild affection, respect, and mutual amusement. And my relative loyalty to that.

Honest: I think that is approximately what we have been having all along, Madam.

Woman: Yes, but under all of that was the promise of something more. What I offer is to remove that promise.

Honest: A more straightforward agreement?
Hmm, the tables turn again. Here I am, reputed for my honesty and lack of pretense, being offered, for the first time in my memory, an honest relation. No trades, no bargains, no deals?

Woman: No.

Honest: So you will, what, "like" me?

Woman: Nothing more.

Honest: And this "liking"…Will I "like " you?

Woman: I don't know. Have you ever liked anyone?

Honest: No.

Woman: Then perhaps you won't. But perhaps you will.

Honest: This is quite fresh. The stakes are so low, it's difficult to know how I would respond. <u>Can</u> I like you?

Woman: Perhaps you would if you could.

Honest: Yes. That's it. I would if I could.

The Interlocutor to the Honest Man

Interlocutor: Ever fuck him?

Honest: Yes.

Interlocutor: And…

Honest: It didn't work out.

Interlocutor: But was it any good?

Honest: …It didn't work out.

The Young Friend and the Woman in Her Boudoir

(*They are sitting quietly together.*)

Young: Am I helping?

Woman: Yes. I am bearing it.

Young: Your loss?

Woman: My love. I am bearing my love.

Young: Oh.

– The End –

Jenny Magnus in *How To Carry Love*

How To Carry Love: A Play with Futon and Bag of Rice

**Premiered 2005
Prop Theater
Chicago, IL**

**Performed by Jenny Magnus
Directed with Stefan Brün**

THE
PLAYS

SETTING

A woman enters with futon on her back. The stage is bare except for a rocking chair to one side. The futon is overwhelming and heavy, covered with white muslin, a moby dick of a futon. She is bent over double to carry it, but she *is* carrying it well. When she reaches the correct place on the stage, she flips it off her back, neat as you please, and it lands with a thud. She fusses it into the correct place, horizontal to the audience, then stands at one end of it, heels against the edge. She prepares, and then flings herself backwards onto the futon, an all-star wrestler's move, falling back on it and slapping her hands on the futon as she hits it, making the impact even greater. She stands up and does this again, several times, practicing the move. She then stops, steps up onto the futon, as if entering a ring, and does not again leave the futon until it is specified.

Angel Wings

There is something I do to men. It's a private little trick that really hooks them in and keeps them invested, intrigued. I grab them by their feet and drag them around on the floor. Their feet are usually very sensitive, and they often have a complex about them, finding them ugly, or stinking, or something to be ashamed about. I hold them tenderly and gain their confidence and gratitude that way. Then I slowly lift their legs and they begin to both tense and relax because they think they're going to get "what they want." So when I start to pull and drag them, it's confusing at first. They really don't know what the hell I am up to. That's when they start to belong to me, that's when they let me in, in that moment of confusion.

Once I know I am really in there, I can speed up. I drag them all around, and the big men in particular are affected, because they have always felt themselves to be too ungainly and monolithic to be moved so fast. And they start to really have fun. They get into the ride. I give them a great ride, whipping them around, sharp corners and momentous arcs. It's the <u>best</u> ride, once they really give in to it.

Then, they start to feel the burn: the rug burn on their back where all their weight has been riding the floor. The pain creeps up, instead of flashing out, and it grows and builds with every passing moment, every inch they are dragged. They can't even perceive it as pain at first because they're having so much fun. But it grows and grows, and soon they are in agony, screaming for me to stop, to let them go. Once I know those burns are deep enough, I do let them go, dropping their feet. They turn over, groaning, trying to feel for the place on their backs where they've been hurt. But the burns are in that one place that you can't reach by yourself, perfectly shaped, healing eventually into scars that forever show anyone who looks at them where those men once had their wings, before they were burned off, cauterized, by me.

A-OK

I have to have it every day. I have to. Have it. Every day. I know some people don't have to, they can go every few days or even weeks or longer. But not me. I have to have it every day. If I don't have it every day, I get very unhappy. If <u>I</u> get very unhappy, you get very unhappy. So for your sake as well as mine, I know I have to have it every day. And I have to have it the way I want it. I have to. Have it. The way I want it. If I don't have it the way I want it, then I haven't had it. And I have to have it. Every day. If I have it the way I want it, then that's fine, I've had it that day. I'm fine. I'm A-OK. And then you're A-OK, and that's what I want. I want everyone to be A-OK. I know some people can have it any old way and still be A-OK, but not me, I have to have it the way I want it, and I have to have it every day, for it to be A-OK. And every day I do have it the way I want it, then it's an A-OK day.

On the days when I don't have it, or it's not the way I want it, I'm not OK. Yes, I'm fine, I function, but I'm not OK. And then I look around and I see other people, and I start thinking, "Did they have it today? Did they have it the way they wanted it?" And I can't get the thought out of my mind that if <u>they</u> had it, and I didn't, then somehow they had it instead of me, they had it and that's <u>why</u> I didn't have it, and that's just wrong. It's wrong because maybe they don't even have to have it every day, but I do. I have to. Have it. Every day. So if they had it and I didn't, it's just wrong, it's not OK. And if it goes a couple of days, and I haven't had it, then I start thinking, where am I going to get it? Am I going to get it from you? Or you? What if you don't want to give it to me? What if you're not willing to give it up so I can have it? What will I have to do to get it? What am I willing to do? Because I know I have to have it. Every day. And I have to have it the way I want it. I have to. And that's the only way, the only way, that I'm ever going to be A-OK.

(The woman is now lying down with her back to the audience, her movements very subtle. This song is recorded, and plays while she moves slowly…)

Red Candles *(sung)*

I had some candles that were red
Dripping into my hot water heater
That could explode at night
The feel of the steam on the back of my neck
As I lay in bed
And on another night
I heard the vicious sounds of growling
And the hot breath of a dog next to my ear
I lay there, adrenal, its presence certain
Till I turned my head
These visitations are happening all the time
Heating and freezing me over
And there's nothing I can seem to do for it

> So if I can I want to make it be
> That I feel the scald of the steam
> Just as the dog is reaching me.

(The woman jumps up, as if waking or suddenly hearing something...She is agitated in the telling...)

Knife in the Back

Oh my god! Oh my god! She didn't even seem to know it. She comes home and it's just sticking out. She's walking around like it's nothing. Like nothing had happened. I'm not even paying attention, and then I notice it. I could see the handle! She's just walking around. So I think, no, it can't be. I look again and it was! The handle of a knife! Sticking out of her back! It was in that one place on your back you can't reach yourself, so of course she can't get it out. I scream, and she stops and looks at me.

(The character pivots back and forth to deliver the two sides of the dialogue.)

What, she goes. I'm like, there's a knife! Sticking out of your back! Oh my god! She goes, I know. And starts just going about her business. I'm like, oh my god! It's a knife! In your back! We have to do something. And she looks at me and she goes, leave it alone. I'm like, leave it alone!? She goes, yeah, don't touch it. It's mine.

So I'm like, ooookkkkk. It's your knife, and you don't want me to touch it. Like, whatthefuck. And she goes, that's right, I want it to stay right where it is. That's where it belongs. I'm like, doesn't it hurt? Aren't you scared? And she goes, yes, and yes, just like that, yes and yes.

So I'm like, fuckingA…fuckinA!? Whatthefuck…fuck…that's fucked. And she goes, that's right. Fucked.

> *(The woman lays down on her stomach, face to the audience, feet upstage. She is like a child, laying on a bed, telling a story…)*

Beauty Place

Everybody wonders where I go. I've got a special beauty place that nobody else knows about. I think everybody ought to have a beauty place. It's not a mirror though. It's not someplace you look at yourself, or even think about how you look. It's not that at all. Mine is on the other side of the line, over along the way I've been told not to, not to, go. Don't go over there! They told me, it's not safe and you could get hurt. But they didn't know I had already been there when they told me that. I found it all by myself.

I fixed it up the way I like it. I found the perfect spot, a place just right, and this is where I come when I want to be beautiful. *(Indicating her spot there on the futon.)* It was hard to hang the rope all by myself. The branch was just right but I had to climb the tree and tie the rope up there. That was kind of scary. But I did it though. Then I dragged the tire here and tied that rope around it. Getting the tire to hang right was really hard because it had to be just the exactly right height. The right height to swing over my back, just at the place I can't reach by myself. It took a long time, but I got it perfect. Then I had to get all the grass off the ground right under the tire. I scrubbed at it with my feet until it was just dirt. Then I lay down on my belly in the dirt and gave the tire a push.

(The woman moves as if the tire is passing back and forth over her back like a pendulum and sending some kind of tremor through her with each pass...)

Everybody ought to have a beauty place. A place to not look at yourself or think about how you look at all. A place to go when you want to <u>be</u> beautiful.

(The woman stands up and repeats the first falling backwards slapping move, making a lot of theatrical noises. For inspiration, watch All Star Wrestling...)

Practice

(Falling moves, speaks in the persona of a tough guy, a wrestler)

Yeah, love. You got to practice love. It don't come "natural." Hate that word. No such thing. You got to practice.

(More falls, flips)

You might think, what's the big deal? Don't look that hard. OK, yeah. It's not hard. It's not hard to love. What's hard is to love right. To not get hurt. And especially, good. To love good. That's what's hard.

(Falls, flips, dives)

OK, like this here? This hurts. OK? But you can <u>take</u> it. You can learn to <u>take</u> it. If you practice.

(Falls)

> *(Falls, gets hurt. Rather than stomp around and curse, he does a little dance and sing-songs the "good mornings.")*

Good morning, good morning, good morning. When I get hurt, I say that. Instead of cursing. Cursing don't get you nothing. It just brings you down. But I had to practice that too. A lot.

Alright, let's break it down.

> *(He steps off the futon and refers back to it as arena, as example, as stage, as platform, as context…)*

OK, love. First, fear. Fear. This is scary. Nothing's there, no guarantees. It's wide open. You gotta know that. Once you know that, then it's just deciding. Am I or ain't I? *("Am I," on the futon; "ain't I," off the futon.)* If you ain't, fine. Don't. Just walk away. If you are, then do it. Don't hesitate, thinkin,' thinkin,' should I shouldn't I should I shouldn't I—go go go.

> *(Huge flipping fall)*

A side note. A lot of noise is helpful. Kind of takes the fear and, uh, expresses it. Out. So it don't stay, in. OK, fear. Then, confusion. Do I, er don't I? *(On and off the futon.)* Really. Yea er nay? Really. Word of advice: don't matter. It don't matter. If you can, you do. If you can't, you won't. So it really doesn't matter what you think. Put it this way: if you find yourself there, doing it, then you do. 'Kay? Simple enough. Just don't get cocky. Remember, this is hard work. But there's a payoff. Didn't think I was gonna get to that, didja? Here's the payoff: after you practice, after you get it goin,' you feel…different. You get a feeling for it, a real deep feeling, like, <u>it's</u> working <u>you</u>. And that is really something. That is something else. Something else again. Yeah, love. That is something. Something else. Again. *(A last flip onto the futon.)*

(The woman lays down on her back, closes her eyes as if to sleep...)

What Abandon Meant (sung)

As with any mystery, there's an answer I don't see
And I don't want to know, don't tell me
I don't want to know
If I had to pick a side, this way run or this way hide
Well I don't want to know, don't tell me
I want to be surprised
I'll close my eyes and take the consequences
Yeah yeah yeah...
Well I have saved and I have spent, thought that's what abandon meant
But now I don't want to know, don't tell me
I don't want to know, I'd rather be surprised
I'll close my eyes and take the consequences
Yeah yeah yeah...

(The woman ends the song rolling back and forth on the futon as if in an intense dream, a wonderful dream of love and pleasure, repeating "yeah, yeah..." like the big affirming YES to all of it...Suddenly, a muslin-covered bag of rice, 18 or so pounds, a miniature of the futon, comes falling down from the ceiling, hits the floor downstage with a thud...

The woman stops rolling around, is startled, gets up, off the futon, and goes and looks at the bag. She might kick it, or poke it, is it going to do anything? She is perplexed by its sudden arrival. She looks back at the futon, and then kind of suddenly decides to sit on the bag of rice, like a little place to perch, a place to hatch?)

The Mother of the Dream *(sung)*

She's the mother of the dream
A symbol to us all
She visits us and licks our butts and licks our wounds
Dries up upside down like grandma's flowers
The complicating malice of the powers that be has she
The mother of the dream
A window to us all
The crowning crack beyond and back
She'll versify the by and by
She's the mother of the dream
A mommy to us all

(The woman realizes at the end of the song that she could still leave, could get out. She begins to sneak off, almost gets offstage, but then thinks better of it, and runs back to gets the bag. She picks it up and it is transformed; she starts carrying it like a briefcase, holding it bunched up in the middle…She is in the persona of an all-business person: a watch, no time, in a hurry, but collected and entitled. Her speech is through a clenched, Hapsburgian jaw…)

Toughie and Bart

I have always loved pets. I had them in my childhood, and then into adulthood. I can just really relate to them, you know what I mean, spiritually. The last pets I had were two cats, a brother and sister team, black cats, named Toughie and Bart. They were as different as night and day, you know what I mean, spiritually. But they were related. Isn't that funny? Bart was the brother, and he was literally a cool cat. He was long and thin, and when you picked him up, he was the kind of cat that would just drape over your hand. He was that relaxed, you know what I mean, spiritually.

He had gotten hit by a car, and had a pimpy limp, and that just added to his coolness. I really just liked him. He ran away.

Toughie was his opposite in every way. Where Bart was relaxed, Toughie was tense. She was short and fat, and looked like a guinea pig. When you picked her up, she would stiffen. Bart would sleep on your neck like a mink stole, and purr and puddle around you. Toughie wouldn't sleep with you, I don't know if she ever slept, she was that tense. Bart had a meow like a yawn, he would say, "meooooow…" Toughie had a meow unlike any I have ever heard, before or since. She would never sit on your lap, but she would follow you around crying "meer, meer, meer…" like that, insistent, it was really annoying.

Then at one point I wanted to move, to San Francisco, Bart had run away by then, and I didn't want to take Toughie, I didn't want to take anything, so I gave her to some friends to watch after. They did, in a way. They left her outside all winter. In Wisconsin. When I came back to visit, I took her to the Humane Society. She got put to sleep. Nobody wanted her. I had a little twinge, you know what I mean, spiritually. I decided I shouldn't have any more pets, that I had used up my chances, karmically. So I never did…

(*As if to leave, then turns back*)…I did just have a baby, though….

> (*The woman is holding the rice bag out in front of her, doesn't know what to do with it, even going so far as to offer it to the audience in a half-assed way. She gets so panicked about where to put it, she finally puts it on her head, where it sits a bit like a hat. The game is to balance it on her head throughout the following…*)

Gave and Got

Oh I gave. I gave as good as I got. And I got a lot, oh yeah, I did, but I gave a lot. Oh yeah. I didn't set out to give that much. No way. I thought, I'll give, like, some. And whatever I get, OK, that's what I get. See, I wasn't even really thinking about getting. I knew I had to give, and I was willing to give, I was, just not as much as it ended up being. Because I gave, then gave more, then more, it never stopped. I couldn't stop giving. Partly it was because of what I was getting. I was getting way more than I had thought I'd get. I hadn't really thought about what I'd get. But I hadn't really thought about how much I'd have to give, either. And once I gave, I gave a lot. I mean, I gave so much, it was gone. And once it was gone, it was gone. What I had to give. That's all there was. So once I gave that, that was it. All gone.

(The bag falls off the woman's head, right at the end. She holds it in the crook of one arm and begins to play it like a drum, patting it in rhythms.)

Evaporation *(sung)*

It's that love shame to blame
That's the way that it looks over the wide open flame
Where it cooks you down to nothing
But the hissing of the spit
Evaporating instantly me

Hold tight onto the tingle if it splinters you
And please don't bite it's the absolutely monarchistic tit
within your vision

And of course you're so right about the
suffocating kisses that envelop
As it twists you, it twists you, twists you

The sweetness is a drug, there's no question
Lies you like a rug, it digests you
Folding you like dough, and then you're patty-caked
Thought you'd like to know, cause no one told me 'bout that

Love shame to blame
That's the way that it looks over the wide open flame
Where it cooks you down to nothing
But the hissing of the spit
Evaporating instantly me

(The woman puts down the bag, bends over with her ass to the audience...)

Ass and Eat

How come the bigger I get, the more invisible I get? You'd think the opposite would be true, but it isn't. I grow, and I shrink. And I know how it happened, oh yes I do....

(She picks up the bag, a delicious thing to nibble on, to tickle...Treacly baby talk, with a vicious edge.)

I like to eat it munchy hug
So nice and sweet
I want to chonk
Mangia mangia
Pinch and poke
Deeeelicious
My little mooga mooga

Have to bite and nip and foof it
Give it to me foot or tush
Gnaw and stuff it
Gladly swallow snarts until I choke
Deeliscious...

> *(The woman spends the last bit of the preceding tying the bag up to a rope that is lowered down. The bag becomes a punching bag, and the persona is a man working out on the bag...)*

Attractive

I am an attractive person. I am. I have always been attractive, not one of those geeks in high school who blooms into an attractive person later on. I was attractive then and I'm attractive now. It's not ego, or anything, that lets me say that, it's just plain fact. No big deal, I'm attractive.

Now my wife, for example, is not attractive. I know, that sounds terrible, but I don't mean I'm not attracted to her, it's just that she's not an attractive person. She's more...repulsive, not ugly, but not...attractive. When you walk into a room, and see my wife and me together, you don't think, wow, that's an attractive couple. You think, he's an attractive guy, and what's her deal? It's plain fact, not a criticism. My wife is not attractive.

One of her problems is how stressed out she is all the time. I say to her, "Honey, what is the big deal? People have been having babies forever, and they don't all melt down and fall apart. Why can't you just get it together and lighten up a little bit?" She doesn't like it when I say that, but hey, the truth is, it's not attractive to be so uptight and exhausted all the time. She hasn't lost the weight, she doesn't take care of herself, and you know what? She looks like she had a baby. She reads those magazines, and I say to her, "Honey, look, Kate Hudson lost the weight, Debra Messing's gonna lose the weight, you can do it if you want to." She doesn't like it when I say that stuff, but being attractive is work. You have to work on it. I work on it, I don't take it for granted, and you know what? I've got more product than she does.

I get home from work, I've been to the gym, I've worked all day, and all I hear about is how hard her day has been. No matter what I'm going through, she's always suffering worse than me. I know it's a juggling act, having a kid and a career, but people do it all the time. She not living in some unique hell of having no time. Nobody has any time. When you're young you don't have enough money and when you get older you don't have enough time, that's true for everybody. She just takes it really hard.

I mean, I have the baby too. She's the hero, she's got the baby, it's all on her, and she's holding up the world. So that's the reason she's not attractive, who's got time to be attractive when they're holding up the world? People don't think about the father having the baby, being just as responsible, I'm holding up the world too, I'm working too, you know what? Sometimes harder than her. But nobody takes that seriously. Or at least they wouldn't forgive me what they forgive her. If I fell apart and lost my mind and couldn't remember anything and got all exhausted and felt like I was always making up for something and being left behind and worrying about the world to the point of being totally depressed, nobody would say, "Yeah, that guy just had a baby, no wonder..." They'd just say, "Whoa, that guy used to be attractive, what happened to him?" I say, "I've been to the gym," and you think, what a selfish prick, he goes to the gym while the poor woman is home with the baby. You know what? I go to the gym. Yes I do. I take showers, I eat decent meals, I get some time for myself. If that's selfish, well, maybe the whole concept of what's selfish ought to be changed. I think its selfish to <u>not</u> take care of yourself and to be shut down and miserable all the time. How is that taking care of your baby? Sacrificing yourself for someone else only leaves that person with a false impression of the world. My baby is going to know how to take care of himself, and not grow up thinking someone is going to do everything for him. Because you know what? Martyrdom is not attractive.

> *(The performer shifts to the persona of an older woman, smoking, whiskey voiced. One arm crossed over her chest, the other with a cigarette dangling between two fingers…)*

Manderley

I don't know how it happened, but suddenly, my daughter is in charge. She's one of these organized types, lists of phone calls and emails to return, she has a little calendar book she's always whipping out. I don't know where she gets all that energy, not from me, I couldn't care less about what day it is or who I'm supposed to be calling back. But she's so fired up, she knows what appointments I've missed before I miss them. And I know she makes some of this crap up, tells me I'm forgetting things. Hey, I saw Rebecca, she's like Mrs. Danvers, killing me with kindness. I don't want to see her go down in a blaze while Manderley burns, but I do wish she'd leave me the fuck alone. Frick. Firk. She's after me about the cursing, says it's one thing to hear it coming out of our mouths, but it's vulgar in a child. And I agree with her. That's the thing, I agree with a lot of what she says, but I hate giving her the satisfaction. The little shit. Shite. Shoot. You know what she said to me the other day? She was looking at me, all squinty and judgmental, and she says, "Ma, you taught me how to nap." And then she leaves it there. So I'm thinking, is that a good thing, er...But it can't be, because of the way she's looking at me. So I think, maybe she hates that because she's too busy to nap now, or cause it unmakes the bed in the middle of the day, or oh hell I don't know. Heck. So I said, "Well, what's wrong with napping, honey?" And I can hear this meekness in my voice, like, don't be mad at me, I know I hurt you, and this is just another way I did, but I don't really understand it so please enlighten me. And that really pisses me off. I mean, OK, I wasn't the greatest mother. I worked, I didn't clean, I got impatient, I was resentful, I wasn't all that happy, I drank, I smoked, but I did the best I could. That's all you can ask of anyone in my opinion. And somewhere along the line she's just going to have to give it a fuckin' rest. Godammit. All of this is going through my mind, and she's looking at me, reading my face. Then she says, "It's just that napping doesn't really help me, ma. It just makes me more tired." "But doesn't it feel good to shut it all out for a while, honey?" She says, "No, because it's all there when you come back." And she's right. The little shit. Shite. Shoot...ah, shit.

> *(The bag is put on the floor, the woman lays down with her head on the bag like a pillow and does not move throughout.)*

Tired

I'm tired. *(Head on bag, long pause)*
Is this boring?...OK, let's play, then.
Let's play...sleep....Too boring?
OK. Let's play stick floating down the river....No?

Let's play Egypt. I'll be the mummy.
Let's play TV. I press the mute button. Shhh, I muted….Dismute?
OK, let's play rug. I'm the rug.
No? How about rock? I'll be the rock.
I'll be the stripe in the middle of the road…
I'll be the black hole…
I'll be dead…Too boring?

> *(The woman stands up with both feet on the bag, at attention. In the persona of a woman in the military, in command, but conciliatory. A motherly apologist for an infantilized people. She speaks in a flat, midwestern accent.)*

Keds, Darlin'

They're keds. They're keds, darlin.' Most of 'em never been away from home before. They aren't thinking straight. What did you do the first time you were away from home? Something gets loosed, let out, mom and dad ain't there, let's party. It's complicated by the fact of them being over here, too. It's not like they're at college, not an overnight visit to a friend or a camping trip. And they're good keds, darlin.' Most 'em are danged good keds. That stupid stuff, well, sad to say it darlin,' it's our fault. They look to us like parents and we failed em…darlin,' yes we did. We let 'em get out of hand and they just did themselves a bunch of stupid stuff. One ked does one thing, someone's got to top him, they're drinkin,' and they're scared, don't forget that, they're scared to death over here. So they do some stupid stuff their parents would be ashamed of, that they're ashamed of, and darlin' it's our fault, oh yes it is. A failure of command, that's what it is, plain and simple, these are keds, they did some stupid stuff, and now they are paying for it.

And those prisoners—did they provoke? It's hard to say, really hard to say what went on. We weren't there, we don't know. The keds say they were provoked, that the prisoners were incommunicado and wouldn't fess up to anything, so they had to do some stuff to them. To get them to talk. OK, they did stupid stuff, but they were just trying to please us, darlin,' trying to do what they thought we wanted. They're good keds! They've been taught to obey their parents. To do what they're told. To try to please them. That's what good keds do. It's the bad ones that disobey. That question everything you say and make you earn every second of attention and respect. So now we have to punish them. The good ones. Who just did what we asked and were trying to please us. Those poor keds.

(The performer holds the bag in her arms like a security blanket. She chews on a corner. The persona is someone very slow, simple in speech, but canny in thought. Always loses their Gs.)

Suck

I like to suck. One of the thins I most like to suck are those sport bottles. I'm glad they invented those, they make sense to drink water out of. You don't just drink it, actually, you suck it. That's what makes it good. I like thins that are like that, that are invented because it makes sense. Some one sat down and thought: people like to suck, and they need to drink, right, so I will make up something that is both of those. At my job, almost everybody uses those sports bottles, actually, almost everybody I know all over uses them.

Most people like to suck, nobody will really admit it or talk it over, but just look at the way people are and you can tell they do. People who smoke are people who like to suck. People who are fat like to suck. Strong he-men type guys like to suck, they are the ones who won't admit it, but somthin tells me they do. At the gym they pump and lift, and then, they suck. It's one of those thins you don't notice until you do notice it and then it's everywhere. When you see a baby with its mama you don't need to think about whether that baby likes to suck, of course it does. And then those bippies or nucks or whatever they call them, the kids like to suck those. And thumbs, that's a big one. But nobody thinks any of that is weird or somthin, they accept that as bein part of childhood. We've all been raised up on sippy cups, right? Even sexyness has suckin in it. It's when you think about how people <u>are</u> anymore, how they are when they grow up, that's when it gets kind of interestin to me.

Like, if people are supposed to be grown up and thinkin about thins differently than kids do, why are they so interested in the dumbass TV shows that make the world seem either like a scary place where someone will save you, or like a fun place where everythin is always OK? It's always one or the other, like the world isn't a place where it's surely both. And how come we know that we are, like, the only people who live on the world who have the time to think about this stuff, because we are the richies, but we snigger or cry about that and won't just admit it flat out? And also how it's no good anymore to use big words, how everythin is made simpler. And I notice how we all just look for papa and mama to come home, and make somthin with sugar in it for us to eat. And how we want someone to tell us when to worry and when to feel good. But we get mad at them for doin it too, just like with mama and papa again. How we still have to hide our face when the witch comes. There seems like there is somthin too hard about just lookin at it, takin it straight, drinkin the last gross part of the drink, where the spit mixes with the grounds.

I personally don't mind drinkin that part, but I like to drink it in my suck bottle. That way it seems sweeter, and there's some control on the flow.

> *(The woman sits down in the chair. The bag is now, finally, a babe in arms. She rocks and coos, and holds the bag as if to nurse it...The persona is a young woman, a new mother, Wisconsonian in accent. Loving...)*

Comfort

Nursing is a very individual experience. You can't really tell how it's going to be for somebody else. For some women it just doesn't work, they can't get into the swing of it, or it hurts too much, or they have to work full time, or they just flat out don't like it. And other people like it a lot and it's easy and no big deal. My little girl calls it "mushy." Isn't that funny? We don't know where she got that from, "mushy." Actually that's a fine thing to call it, one friend of mine told me before I had my little girl to be careful what I called it cause if you nursed long enough they were going to talk about it. She told me how they called it "booby" and her little daughter yelled out one time, "mommy I want booby, I want booby," and they were in church. Kind of embarrassing. I know some people say that if the child is old enough to ask for it, it's time to stop. But I think, why take that away from them if they still get something out of it. I mean, sure it's not for food anymore, but for comfort. And I just don't know how much comfort there is in this world anymore.

I think a lot about this one family I used to work for. Before I had my little girl I was one of those in-home nurse assistants, you know, who go in and help take care of people who are sick at home. Sometimes you clean them up, or make a meal for 'em, or just sit there with them until somebody else comes. This one family had a sick mother, she was dying, and sometimes that's a real slow thing that the family has time to get used to and then they aren't as upset, in a way. This family was still real real upset, it wasn't something they were used to at all, I don't know the particulars, but I think it was kind of sudden.

So they had her in this downstairs area, with a hospital bed right up next to the windows so she could look out at the yard and the trees. They were there with her all the time, at least one of them, helping her, talking to her, but mostly just sitting with her, crying. There was a husband and 3 grown up kids. Two of the kids came and went a lot, but one of them was there all the time. She had her husband there with her and their little baby, who couldn't have been more than a couple months old. She would sit on this couch they had pulled up to the bed, and she would nurse her little baby and rock her and sing to her, and keep her mother company at the same time. It was just real real sad. I mean, it was always sad, someone dying, but something about that baby coming, right at the same time as the grandma was going, that was sad.

Well, one time, I came over to go to work, and I would just let myself in the front door, that was how they liked it, in case the mother was sleeping. I came in, and I heard some singing, so I thought, oh that daughter is sitting with her little baby, but when I came around the corner, I saw that the daughter was sitting on the bed, holding up the mother in her arms, kind of had her in her lap. And she was nursing her. I had a real weird feeling when I saw it, it was kind of gross and scary, but I didn't make any noise, I just backed back out of the room. And the daughter was singing this little song, just 2 notes over and over, like they call it, crooning, "ahhhh ahhhh…ahhhh ahhhh…" Just like that over and over.

At that time, I remember very well kind of judging her, the daughter. I even thought, I wonder if I should report this to someone, cause sometimes people use up their loved ones' drugs and stuff, and you have to protect them, the sick ones. I mean, isn't that like, incest or something? And the picture of her, her big old breast, a vein running through it, and that old lady, cradled in her arms like that, it stayed with me for a long time. I had to quit that family after that, I didn't want to think about whether that had happened before or if was just the once, or what, so I never went back there. Eventually that picture faded and I forgot about it.

Then, when I had my little girl, and I nursed her, it came back to me sometimes. I guess it kind of makes sense to me now. People just need comfort sometimes, you know? And if you love them, you want to give it to them.

The Empty Nest *(sung)*

Though you have to go
And though I love you so and want what's best for you

Please don't leave me now

Cordially invited to remain
Restraining all the little impulses to heartsick you
Give me extra room inside your brain
Remember me remember me remember me
The way I've promised to remember you

Though you have to go
And though I love you so and want what's best for you

Please don't leave me now

This is the lap we've made
Carved out all the hollows till it fits you well
A lavish price we've paid
Forever more more more
There's always more for me to tell, about you

Though you have to grow
And though I love you so and want what's best for you

Please don't leave me now
Some other day
Just please don't leave me now…

(Lights fade slowly on song…)

– *The End* –

Jenny Magnus in *Room*

Room

**Premiered 2007
Prop Theater
Chicago, IL**

**Performed by Jenny Magnus
Directed by Stefan Brün**

Room

SETTING

The performance takes place in a room. The set is a large projection screen upon which, rear projected, is a picture of the room the performance takes place in, and a plain chair set in front of the screen. The performer is sitting in the audience as the audience enters, watching, smiling, being present with them as they settle in their seats.

The image on the screen begins as a wide shot of the stage, and gradually changes during the course of the performance, subtly dissolving into ever closer views of the stage, close up photographs of the floor, the walls, the material of the room, until, at the end, the images are wholly abstract, so zoomed in that the walls and floor become landscapes in themselves, and the feeling of vast scale and intense detail take over any recognizable aspect of the room. The performance is accompanied by recorded musical arrangements, to which the performer sings live. The chair is a place to sit, nothing more. Or perhaps a place of comfort, and being apart from it breeds anxiety.

(A pause while the audience settles, then the lights cross-fade from house to theater lighting. The performer would like to start but something is holding her back...She begins the monologue from her seat in the audience.)

(Finally turning her attention to the audience—is it their fault?)

Stop doing anything. Stop right now. Just sit there. Or, don't even do that. Don't think, don't prepare, don't imagine or envision, don't defend or expect or...just stop...and I will too...Or, I won't either...So. *(A long pause)*

We're all here, right now, all of us. Together in this room. That's a fact...

(A sudden thought. She jumps up from her seat and takes a place on the stage to make her point.)

But what if we weren't? What if we had been struck, or, what if the world just suddenly winked out, a sudden sweeping off our feet, but no time of sweeping, just one moment there and the next moment, not there. Rather, not here, not in this room...What if this room were absolutely empty? Austere, arid, but not in a bad way, emptiness like a great relief, a literal relief. No sound but the wind, no animals or bugs, like a different planet or a desolate, decimated, leveled place, but not in a bad way, a place that felt right, like being in the right place. What if being here, being in a desolate place, felt like being in the right place? *(Pause)*

Then I would want to tell you something...

Ordinary Life (sung)

I seen the hills outside Salinas California
And they were rolling amber waves of grain
Perfectly round, perfectly still, like a body in sleep
Except for the cows, or maybe a tree, on top of the hill
All gnarly and free...
It was one of those moments
That I'd been waiting for
One of those moments
Well worth waiting for through years of blindness and despair...
At a bus stop in Madison Wisconsin
A certainty occurred to me
Each of us dies, no one is spared, not even the young,
in spite of their hopes,
Their loves or their lies,
It makes living life so simple and free...
It was one of those moments
That I'd been waiting for
One of those moments
Well worth waiting for through years of blindness and despair...
See mine's an ordinary life
Others can see so much farther than me,
I've always known that's true
But every now and then
Something <u>real</u> shines through...

(Performer finishes singing, stands neutrally, just being there...works on neutrality, has to keep finding and losing it...)

I don't mind breathing. I kind of like it. I'm annoyed by having to make myself remember breathing, but I guess I even don't mind that, being annoyed. When I'm breathing, I feel more alive, more living, than when I have forgotten. It's more stressful to breathe, forgetting is so easy, you relax, actually. Just relax and don't bother. It's bothering to breathe that causes all the stress, because once you breathe, then you have to live, and that's a huge problem. All that awareness, the consciousness, the being present, the attention, thinking about your spine, your shoulders, your neck, other people, it's a hassle. But something about it does appeal, in an experiential kind of way. I am interested in experience, in the experience of breathing, it's oddly interesting to me, in a way, couldn't tell you why, it's just appealing. There's a lot of reasons to be annoyed by it, put out, but what if, somewhere along the way, you just have to accept you have an interest in it, in breathing, in living, you have to embrace it, even if it is annoying or stressful or troublesome…

System Song (sung)

Wake up slow no place to go
Wake up super everything's a stupor
Wake relieved not to be believed
Wake up distraught tells you that you're caught
Wake up tired that's right you're retro-fired…
<u>What</u> is the system?
What <u>is</u> the system?
What is the <u>system?</u>
Wash your face without a place
Wash your hand remove the brand
Wash your head relax instead
Wash your crotch knocks you down a notch
Wash your ass take a needed pass…
<u>What</u> is the system?
What <u>is</u> the system?

What is the <u>system?</u>
Pick the clothes nobody knows
Pick the meal tells you how to feel
Pick the route try to be astute
Pick the spot in spite of what you brought
Pick the time for you the bells do chime…
<u>What</u> is the system?
What <u>is</u> the system?
What is the <u>system?</u>
Psssttt…lemmee whisper…
Dimwit mandatory observations
of an orchestrated catastrophe….

(Annoyed, answering a query that hasn't been asked…)

Don't say there isn't a form, there's a fucking form, for crap's sake, you don't perceive it maybe, but it's fucking there. The random aspects of detail, if nothing else, the particular characteristics of every specific aspect and component part of this circumstance, right now, and somebody has to pay attention to it. Somebody has got to give it their good attention. Or so what? Huh? So what if Fame never made a bed? Maybe Fancy never cooked a supper, OK? Superior never rocked a baby, Special never hung up wash, Perfect never cleaned the floor, Number One never read a bedtime story, Newsworthy never paid the bills, Headliner never fixed the sofa, Interview never wiped a butt…and if they never did any of those things, who did? Huh? Who does all the stuff that needs doing, when there is so much to pay attention to? I know, I know…pointy boot lickers need pointy boots. Sure, sure, fancy spoon gaggers need fancy spoons. Resentful ass kickers need resentful asses. You know, to kick…So yeah, but what if sorcery doesn't work anymore? What if exercises don't work anymore? What if frantic doesn't work anymore, organized doesn't work anymore, cornflakes don't work anymore, random access doesn't work anymore, removal doesn't work, moron thoughts don't work, haplessness doesn't work, formulas don't work, crashing doesn't work, instinct doesn't work, prayer doesn't work, frozen lips don't work, what if nothing works?

(Woozy, drunkish, a center of gravity problem...)

Frank's Room *(sung)*

One more bad thing, one more big bad thing
That's when he would wake himself up,
is after one more bad thing...
Frank lived in a crummy little room
He decorated it after a crummy sphynxy tomb
The only way he kept his bed was as a
grave kept for the dead...
His rug was stained with gravy drips
And filled with lots of toenail clips
And when he picked up his clothes
The creatures underneath them froze...
One night he lay down on top
And thought the spin would never stop
But when he put his foot down on the floor
It only spun round all the more...
His eyeballs lived inside a box
That crossed when he would grip his cock
His haircut grew out long at night
And stuffed the pillow much too tight...
He dreamt his version of a heavenly bliss
Standing and pissing a golden piss
That emptied him so flat and clean
His kneecaps bent but didn't lean

> He lifted himself above the rim
> And looking down he dived straight in
> Breathing thick and holding true
> He swam up pipe and then he flew
> One more bad thing, one more big bad thing
> That's when he would wake himself up, is after
> one more bad thing…

(Still drunkish) …I really like you. I like you so much. Audience.

> *(A name, the person being talked to, confidentially confided in, maybe inappropriately, maudlin… directly speaking to the audience.)*

The other day, I sat in here, in this room, and I had an imaginary conversation with you. Just you and me in here, in this room, together, only you weren't here, you were imaginary. And I spoke my truth to you, I did, I spoke it, I said, I like you, I really, really like you Audience, I fear you, yes, but I like you. I like your faces, I like having you here with me, together in this room, I feel like I have something to give you, I said this to you when you weren't really here, I said, Audience, we've known each other for such a long time, I am so much more at home, here, with you, so much more present, than in my real life, than when we aren't here together, and you didn't answer, you just let me go on, so I said, Audience, I kind of love you, in my way, I do, and I hate you too, you piss me off, with your fickly attention withholding, with your needs and your shifting hierarchies of condemnation… *(Sobering up)* and I thought, I'm of two minds. One the one hand, I want connections with people, true love towards god and man, to be of service, to live a life based on humility, kindliness, tolerance, and love. I want orchidy thought, cultivated, rarified, prized above all. Doing for myself what I would have <u>you</u> do, the zennyest zen simplicity of purple lit red love rooms, full of secret treasured glamorized sex explosions and alice-ish spelunking adventures ending up in alternate universes, fully peopled, filled with light. I want all that, Audience.

On the other hand, I hate everyone and I want to be left alone in my room with my treats, my drugs, my booze, my pornos, my iPod Touch, the phone off, the door locked, the window shades down, left to my own devices, no more effort, no more caring, no more energy, no more love, no more interest, no more crap eating anxious worm sounds or half assed incoherent erstwhile ham handed arguments, smack rage or red faced slap happy dormant stoplights, just left alone to <u>be</u> scared, <u>be</u> weak, have no faith, live alone in it, and <u>be</u> ashamed…So you see, I am of two minds…

King of Tomorrow (sung)

Sitting pretty catbird seat
Lucky ducky golden feat
Smells like roses filled with jam
The King of Tomorrow I am I am
The smallest speck a teensy drop
Leftover crusts to a sudden stop
A dirty rug a constant buzz
The King of Tomorrow I was I was…
I know I am fortunate and that is part of my good fortune
I am wealthy beyond all measure and that is part
of my good fortune
I have wealth and fortune because I have wealth and fortune
and that is certainly a big part of my good fortune…
Plant a garden ride the wave
Opening presents the smoothest shave

> Criminal beauty to a touchdown slam
> The King of Tomorrow I am I am
> Except I'm bug infested a drooped bouquet
> Dirty dishes on a rainy day
> Fat and gassy a moldy fuzz
> The King of Tomorrow I was I was…
> I know I am not fortunate and that is part of my misfortune
> I am poor in spirit and that is part of my misfortune
> My poverty of spirit and misfortune stems from my poverty of spirit and misfortune and that is most certainly a big part of my misfortune…

(A renewed resolve, a call to arms…)

So, what is the <u>least</u> I can do? Because I am conserving my momentum…I'm on an intermissionary exodus, so I'm not going to worry about something like damage, or idioms of distress, no, my position is Masada…All of us, together, here in this room, a siege, on a plateau, we must decide our fates, we wait… we attend…

(A long pause, then breaking out of the drama to address the strategies involved.)

OK, now right here, in the show, I can perform order perceived as chaos, or chaos perceived as order… *(Aware that the audience cannot make this choice)* Oh don't say it, I know, I know…the problem with an existential exploration of the problem of being is that it is very <u>problem</u> oriented…

But let's sincerely ask ourselves this question…if our subject is attention…What if we were sitting in a room where the wall next to which we were sitting was separating us from the explosive tumult of a teardown happening 2 feet from where we were sitting in a room that was quiet except for the sounds of the teardown happening 2 feet from where we were sitting? To be sitting so close to the sounds of destruction in a quiet room that is not being torn down but that is being shaken by the tearing down of a room 2 feet from where you are sitting and thinking that at any minute the wall next to which you are sitting must also surely be destroyed, <u>is</u> sitting in invisible destruction, happening all around you (without dust or evidence), except for the sounds and the possibilities from the wall next to which you are sitting…

String of Pearls *(sung)*

She'd set up her suspicions in a row
Then the instinct for typhoon would start to blow
Her floating mind like an old duck blind
Hiding worries under camouflage
String of pearls
Where did she get them
String of pearls
A tender heirloom
She'd stopped blinking right round the time she left
Her kitchen counter cluttered and bereft
The strangest part of her tantrumy heart
Was not to hate the thief and not to hate the theft
A string of pearls
How did she make that
String of pearls
Her tender heirloom
She was staying right with it
One pearl at a time…

Her days were short and full of price tags
She broke her failures like a sight gag
With a banished ache for the will to take
The shortcuts that got her lost again...
A string of pearls
How does she make that
String of pearls
Her tender heirloom...
By staying right with it
One pearl at a time
She'll be staying right with it
One pearl at a time....

(To the audience, as clearly as possible...It all comes down to this...)

We are all here together in this room right now. And I want to tell you something I have learned in all my long years, Audience. Nobody is going to save us. And we aren't going to save anybody. The cleaning lady is not coming. And if our subject is attention, and while we consider all there is to pay attention to, both in this room and outside, right next door, both good and bad, Audience, because that is the nature of attention, it swings both ways, it strikes me that paying attention is not a given at all. I can use my personal charisma to try to <u>make</u> you pay attention to me, or to anything—and yeah, I'm the one up here, all the lights are shining on me...Or, you can decide to pay attention. It's your decision to make...And isn't it more interesting that way? Regardless, here we are, right now, in this room, all together. <u>That</u> might be something to pay attention to.

(During this song, the performer moves back and forth between being in the audience and being on the stage.)

All Together (sung)

We are all here together, all of us right now together
And we all are looking at the stage right now
That is why we are together, all of us in this room together
And not home alone with the radio
Stories can be told in a million different ways
And stories can be sold in about a million different ways
But it's attention we all share with what we see up there
And that is something that can never be recreated
unless we're all right here together
We are all here together, all of us right now together
And we all are looking at the stage right now
That is why we are together, all of us in this room together
And not home alone with the radio…

(Music plays out, performer goes back to sitting in the audience… Projected images are of the most macro zoomed-in close ups of the room, to the point where they are unrecognizable textures. The lights cross-fade from theater lights to house lights…)

– The End –

Jenny Magnus in *Nowhere But Up*

Nowhere But Up

**Premiered 2009
The Viaduct for RhinoFest
Chicago, IL**

**Performed by Jenny Magnus
Directed by Stefan Brün**

SETTING

A television is on a dark stage. It is raised to eye height, on a pedestal, higher than a table. The television comes on, a blue, flickering set of collaged images, not comprehensible rationally, but emerging as a portrait of old age in a nursing home, a confused, dementia-inspired flow of fractured impressions, seen through a quiet chaos of insensibility. Images of trees outside windows, of the metal legs of a wheelchair, of ancient feet, of old messed up legs, of bedclothes, of hallways... Also, silhouettes, light coming through a window shining on a pillow, a strange shadow of a face, head in hands...

A woman enters quietly, watching the TV. She is sad, defeated, but present. She turns to the audience, acknowledges them, sighs, then takes a stance with both arms raised, one at right angle to her body, as if she is going to perform a big, old fashioned theatrical song. Like a runner takes their position before they start a race, she gears up mechanically, without much joy, but ready to begin.

Music begins. The song is Kurt Weill's "There's Nowhere to Go But Up." The introduction plays, and just before the vocal comes in, a slap can be heard. The woman reacts as if the slap hit her in the face. She is hurt, dismayed, but then the vocal starts, and she is jogged into action. She suddenly realizes there is work to be done, and as the song plays, she exits the stage, re-enters with a wooden rocking chair. She places it next to the television, so that it is just over the shoulder of whoever would be sitting in the chair. But this requires a bit of finesse and fussing, and the woman is all anxious repositioning, even going into the audience to check the placement. She is filled with nervous energy, and only stops fussing when the lyric gets to the tag line, "...There's nowhere to go but up." She sings along live to the rest of the song, harmonizing, and trying to live up to the wildly optimistic message of the song, but ultimately failing. She is whistling in the graveyard.

She relates to the chair throughout as if it were a person— an elderly, incapacitated person, hard of hearing, needing care, and she is troubled by the thought of the person being uncomfortable or unhappy. The chair and the television are the whole world of the stage. It all comes down to this, a small area of light in a large world of darkness. The song finishes, a desperate flourish, the woman is in the "ready to sing" position, arms raised at right angles to the body, again presentationally signaling her intention to perform. Then she drops the stance as she speaks...

She's going...she's going...and she cannot be portrayed. At least, I cannot portray her...(*A thought*) But, if I were to portray her, this is how I would portray her:

(She sits in the chair, very consciously and deliberately taking a position of someone incapacitated, one hand curled up, the other gripping the armrest, body slumped. Go visit any nursing home and the position is instantly clear.)

(A voiceover begins, a sing-songy condescension of false reassurance, the institutional version of "caring" tones, spoken by someone for whom English is a second language.)

Come on Barbie, let's get ready for bed...
Oh watch out Barb it's slippery on that floor...
Bar-bar-a have you eaten your lunch yet...
Barb! Don't stand up without locking...
No, no, now Barbie, that's nighttime medication...
I'm here, I'm here, Barb, stop pushing the button...
You're not the only one who's suffering here Bar-bar-a...

("Bar-bar-a" repeats monotonously. The woman is listening to the voice, and growing increasingly agitated. She may be incapacitated, but she is not an idiot. Her voice grows louder, and more angry.)

Motherfuckers, motherfuckers...
MOTHERFUCKERS!!!

(The song is sung live, with pre-recorded accompaniment. The text is delivered in a singing speech, as if being thought in the moment. The woman portrays the person in the chair, who is trying to stay focused on what is happening. She addresses the audience, grows nervous because she cannot quite keep it all together.)

Inventory Song   (sung)

There's something of value in taking an inventory
Of knowing the things you need and what you've got
But then those categories can get mixed up
And all you're left with is multiple lists that are growing
and shrinking and not very helpful…

But here goes:

There's twinkly lights in the window
There's a little girl on my lap sometimes
There's family pictures taped up
I guess they're reminders of where I'm at
There's a stink and pads in the bathroom
There are scabs and bruises and pain
The cigarettes and scarves and going outside
Then the day seems over but then you do it again…

There's a TV and many WWII documentaries
Which seem vaguely familiar but then again, not
There's a tray at mealtimes but mostly the food is awful
There's a lot of Kleenex and snot and wait a minute
let me catch up

There is the feel of a hospital but no one is really a doctor
There are people out in the hall who are screaming my name,
I think

There are pills and protein drink and something else
they put in a cup
I'm supposed to be taking it but I've been hiding it waiting
for the right moment to take it all at the same time (ha!)

There's this green pad thing they make me sit on
It beeps if I try to stand up
I think that I must be in a foreign country because I can't
understand anyone here
But that doesn't seem right because I don't remember going
anywhere in particular…

There's my daughter who comes to see me every day
She brings oranges and candy and her little daughter,
and oh! That's who sits on my lap
There's a drip in the ceiling whenever it rains
that makes me very angry
And there's one guy in particular that wants to give me a
shower but I would rather have a woman

There is one piece of my own furniture
I don't know why that thing is here
Because it seems like it should be back at home with
everything else
Unless, wait a minute, I think… oh god, we <u>sold</u> that house…

There's some crackpot who comes in every once in a while
Who tells me some crap I don't recall
There are lots and lots of people
who call me by the wrong name
I don't know why they don't understand me when I correct
them again and again

There are some little twinkly lights up in the window
I think it might be around Christmas time

There's somebody out in the hallway
and they might be calling my name
There's another tray of food and the TV is on again,
or is it, still?

Oh when am I going to get out of here?
When will I walk decently again?
When can I die, I am not afraid
I would rather be dead than go on with this charade

What is my reason for living at this point?
Who can help me just stop?
Ah, what good is this list anyway?
Now I'm just pissed off.
Fuck it, fuck this, fuck fuck fuck!...

Occasionally I like to take an inventory
Trying to keep track of something, but
I think it's getting harder to stay on the subject...
Hey who put those twinkly lights up in my window?
They're pretty.....

(The woman pivots out of the character of the person in the chair, back into herself...)

(To audience) Now, you didn't think I was going to leave you with <u>nothing</u>, did you?

(She physically pivots out of the chair and squats down as if to speak to the person in the chair, loudly, slowly, as if to someone who is having difficulty understanding...)

YOU DIDN'T THINK I WAS GOING TO LEAVE YOU WITH NOTHING, DID YOU?

(She pivots again, this time back to the audience.)

Well, did you? I wouldn't leave you with <u>nothing</u>...No....

(She steps forward and a light is added to the space, closer to the audience, outside of the world of the chair and the television.)

Dream of driving in a huge camper/truck with Bab. She is both driving and on the phone, then I am on the phone hearing a message from Ralph, who is dead, but also operating the gas and the brakes with my hands. I decide I have to take control, so I crawl over Bab to get into the driver's seat. We are in Europe somewhere, she is absurdly spray tanned on her legs in shorts, which seem strong and beautiful, if really, really tan. She is anxious but willing to have me drive. She is harping on and on about what the doctor said and how full of shit he was, I get into the seat in time to narrowly avoid an accident and we pull into a little area out of traffic. I turn to her and really talk to her and tell her it's alright to accept that it's the end and that we can have a lovely time together being close and traveling and looking at things, and just as it seems I am about to convince her, suddenly Julie is on the phone, telling me that she and Greg have moved all of Bab's stuff out of her home and when she comes back she is going to live at "Pancake," which I don't quite know what that means, but it seems terribly underhanded to have done it that way. Julie is frantic and contrite on the phone, and then I am at "Pancake," which is a nursing home, of course. I am in Bab's room on the shitty phone there and I cannot get Bab to hear me, she is evidently in Oslo, and I just want her to understand that she should wait there for me and I will come to her there, but I can't be sure she is hearing me or tracking me and I am yelling into the phone while her roommate and the administrators and people visiting other people in the nursing home look on...

(Heavy sigh)
She cannot be portrayed. At least, I cannot portray her...

(Thinking)
Now, but, if I were going to portray her, this is how she would have me portray her...

(The woman takes a stance of an aristocrat, a cigarette in hand, someone accustomed to giving orders. She is happily choosing something with her "yes's", and denying something with her "no's." The yes's and no's are on opposite sides of the stage, she is positioned to give her back to that which she is saying no to. The dichotomy becomes increasing insistent, as if her wishes are not being granted. She becomes almost desperate at the last, the fear creeping in as she says "no" again...Not quite a shriek, that would be gauche, but it is dawning on her that the situation is not entirely
within her control.)

Yes...No...Yes!
No...no. Yes, yes yes...NO.
No, no.

(Music starts, a welcome distraction. An organ plays, it is sentimental. The images on the television are of a blazing red and orange sunset, the tone of the song is Vera Lynn "Till We Meet Again"-ish, a stiff-upper-lip of ennobled suffering, of self-pity, which cracks occasionally, and the real sentiment, rage, surfaces. The woman begins the song in the "ready to sing" position, all her demeanor is in the grand tradition of the music playing as the Titanic sinks...)

The Old Heave-a-Roo *(sung)*

I've lived a life like many do
With ups and downs, I've had a few
Things have a way of coming round
And bringing you right back to where you started
Doesn't it seem to be completely a propos
That I should be here telling you these things, just so?

Let's give it the old heave-a-roo, heave-a-roo
Give it the old heave-a-roo
I'm sorry my dear for the pain and the fear
I gave my best to you

And if we could say goodbye
Though we may cry
That's all there is to that
And there may come a time
When you may find
Yourself, sitting right where I once sat *(gestures to chair)*
(Rage) Believe me

(Returns to Vera Lynn) I'm tired of trying to explain
Seduce cajole again and again
It seems you fail to understand
Being lost alone and brokenhearted
Wouldn't it seem to be completely a propos
If we could find some way to bring the end, just so?

Let's give it the old heave-a-roo, heave-a-roo
Give it the old heave-a-roo
I'm sorry my dear for the pain and the fear
I gave my best, goodbye, *(rage)* good luck to you…

> (The last note is held for as long as possible, even as it deteriorates, the woman in the "ready to sing" position and straining forward, holding on long after the time to let the note go has come and gone…Finally, when she is out of breath, she drops the stance…)

She's going…she's going…and she cannot be portrayed. At least, I cannot portray her…
Now, if I am not going to portray her, this is how I would <u>not</u> portray her…

> (The woman sits in the chair, back into the position of the incapacitated person. She is grim, determined to show how <u>not</u> to portray her…)

> (Angry, very angry, looking around, things are not alright. Someone is going to pay…)

Where is she? Where the fuck is she?! What is going on? This is crazy. This is a shit ass way to end things. I fucking hate old people. Where the fuck is she? She doesn't care. She's dumped me, she doesn't like it when I say that, but tough shit, it's true. I'm dumped here, she's not here, he's not here, fuck them. They don't know, really, they don't care. She's here occasionally. Whenever she can be. She tells me, "I'll be here when I can, and when I can't, I won't. I'm doing my best." Doing her best…I just bet she's doing her best. But it's not good enough. That's what I tell her, I say, doing your best? It's not good enough. You have to do something, fix this, right now, I mean it, I am not kidding around, this is impossible. Doesn't she care about that? But she doesn't. She doesn't do anything, she tells me a lot of bullshit, everybody is full of bullshit. Got it all figured out, earnest, good arguers, willing to fight, but she doesn't do anything, nothing changes, no matter what I say, I have tried and tried to tell her, to describe what this is like for me, to make her understand, but she just listens. I know it's hard for her. But it's not harder for her than it is for me, it's not even close. I tell her that, that I know it's hard for her, but it's…it's not even close, for Christ's sake! I would trade her any day. She says she knows I'm suffering and she's sorry but there's nothing more she can do, there's nothing more anybody can do. Come on, nothing more she can do! That's what she says! As if she's done anything! What has she done? What have any of them done? I'm still here. She's not here, where is she? What is she doing? What about my, my, my…civil rights? I fought my whole life for freedoms! What is going on!!??? Don't leave me before I'm gone! This is crazy.

> *(The woman sits forward, leaves the character of the incapacitated person, addresses the audience.)*

Attention must be paid…Because she's going…she's going…

> *(The woman experimentally tries her hands in the claw positions that the incapacitated person has, sadly observing the movement back and forth between claw and neutral hand. Music starts, and she then slowly slips back into the chair, into the incapacitated position, only this time, she is staring, drooly, even more far gone… She comes back enough to sing…Eventually, in the song, she stands up and enacts a slow motion perpetual falling, arms outstretched almost in the "preparing to sing" position, but this time, like windmilling, falling arms, slowly flying down, not able to catch or arrest the falling, but delaying it for a moment, maybe?)*

Falling (sung)

I used to believe
That I could receive
I used to believe in love
But now I believe in the ticking down of…

She's always falling
waking up falling
sitting down falling
standing up falling
sorrow falling failing falling
catching slipping falling
cutting falling freaking falling
loving her out of it falling
failure falling pathetic falling
gifts and treats and trying falling
not being able to flat faced falling
confusedly falling
succor and comfort and lostedly falling
Christmas and birthday and old man's meal falling
dismay falling
ready to be done with it all falling
stop that stop that falling…

(Sitting again, but as herself)
I used to believe
That I could retrieve…
I used to believe in love
But now I believe in the slipping down of…

(One last time, as the incapacitated person, a last, most desperate cry...)

DON'T LEAVE ME BEFORE I'M GONE!

(As herself, angry, sad, it's all too much, there is no answer...)

Don't be <u>gone</u> before you're gone.

(Sitting back, relaxed in the chair, it's all over, really, but the shouting...Singing again.)

I used to believe in love. But now...

(The woman rocks slowly in the chair, the music stutters out, the light slowly fades, all that is left is the television. An image of a silhouette on a pillow, light shining in through a window: a face, some vertical strips of shadow that look like bars of a cell. The figure grips the bars, there is no escape... the television blips out.)

– *The End* –

Still in Play: A Performance of Getting Ready

Premiered 2011
Museum of Contemporary Art
Chicago, IL

Performed by
Nia Amandes, Jayita Bhattacharya,
Jeffrey Bivens, Briana Finnegan,
Sidonie Greenberg, Judith Harding,
Cat Jarboe, Jenny Magnus, Troy Martin,
Beau O'Reilly, Colm O'Reilly,
Matt Rieger, John Starrs,
Matt Test, and Vicki Walden
Directed by Stefan Brün
Assistant Directed by Jennifer Moniz

< Jenny Magnus and H.B. Ward in *Still In Play*

Still in Play: A Performance of Getting Ready

is intended as a portrait of a theater ensemble. In the stagings thus far, that ensemble has been the Curious Theatre Branch, of which I am a founding member. The first production of this play was commissioned by The Museum of Contemporary Art in Chicago, as the culmination of my year-long residency there. As the production—a hybrid of ensemble-devised work and the creations of one writer's mind—came into being, the Curious ensemble was able to address and, to a certain extent, exorcise some of the demons we have faced over our 25 years in existence. The themes and ideas in *SIP* are, in a way, a result of group autobiography, and we approached the making of this work as an experiment in self-reflection.

This being said, *Still In Play (SIP)* stands as an open invitation to any other ensemble to create a portrait of themselves, using these texts and ideas as a template. All performing groups have some things in common: the tension between belonging and separation, power dynamics and talent differentials, the struggle to make something out of nothing, and the mechanics of the creation of theater. My intention with this script is to challenge ensembles to self-reflection, to create their own portrait of how <u>they</u> "get ready."

There are sections in the play spoken by the "Stage Manager," which can be the actual stage manager, or an actor portraying a stage manager. I wrote these texts to reflect the spaces we were performing in: The Museum of Contemporary Art and later, Links Hall. I am intimately familiar with both these spaces, and had a strong sense of what made them singular. I invite you to write texts that tell the poetry of the spaces you perform in. I am interested in having the most poetical texts in the play spoken by the one "non-actor"—the technician—who says them as part of the process of focusing lights, testing microphones, or in some way riding the line between being "real" in the play and real in the world. This razor-sharp divide is where the whole play should live: the real moment of people talking about what is happening, and the "real" moment of a composed, performative act. How these realities can play out at the same time is of the highest interest and excitement to me. Other moments in the play can tease the audience with this: the fight, the warming ups, the rehearsal of texts, the soliloquies, the entering of space, the phone call—any and all of this should feel real <u>and</u> "real."

The order of the speeches and dialogues should not be considered sacrosanct. They should at the very least overlap somewhat, so that the audience's attention is challenged: what <u>should</u> they be looking at or listening to? I took as my inspiration here Robert Altman, whose use of a crowded frame with a lot going on leaves to the audience the choice of what is the most important thing in the narrative at a particular moment. The theme of attention—how we give it, desire it, get it—is among the most important in this play. In film, of course, it is possible to use a densely composed soundtrack to carefully bring some sounds to the foreground, and in that way suggest the primacy of a chosen narrative. In our production at the MCA, we used microphones hung from the ceiling and a mix of recorded sound to help create the sense of certain scenes coming out to the forefront and then again being submerged. This was an interesting experiment, but not altogether successful. I encourage you to try it, and let me know how you did it…

The space itself should be empty, or filled with whatever you as an ensemble need in order to get ready. Curious used a table of snacks, a makeup table, a clothes rack, a band set-up, and a simple table and chair, all as "stations" where people congregated and spoke together, or just stood around. These props and set pieces were all brought on by performers at the beginning of the play, as part of the getting ready, and then removed at the end, because the event being prepared for was about to begin. In our productions, the only station pre-set was the single chair and table, where the Solitary Person, who enters the space first, sits, mostly alone and quiet throughout. This character is one of the few that are specific personae—the others being the Stage Manager and the Rehearsing Person. The Rehearsing Person has a few brief lines, which he or she speaks again and again throughout the play, struggling to get them right and delivering them in all the ways one does while rehearsing: with help; perhaps dramatically; and, in the end, simply, to the audience.

All the other characters are open to interpretation. There should be a mix of genders, as some of the issues raised have to do with childcare and sexual arousal, and particular ways men and women experience these things. The songs, in our production, were performed live on stage by the band The Crooked Mouth, whose members are all part of the Curious Theatre Branch ensemble. This was meaningful in our production; it may or may not be in yours.

You will need a minimum of five people to fill all the roles in the play. Maximum number: sky's the limit. We worked with 13. The songs are available on my website; they can be used as recorded by me and The Crooked Mouth, or you can sing them yourself, or write your own. We employed certain movements and activities (happening during spoken scenes and in some cases as scenes unto themselves) to render visible elements of our ensemble's psychology. I have described these below—feel free to use them, or to make up your own.

Still in Play: A Performance of Getting Ready was created as a love letter to our gang, the Curious Theatre Branch. I cannot envision any reason to work with an ensemble for 25 years unless it is based on love. Various notions of the tribe, the gang, the group, the clan, the ensemble, were a big part of our discussion, because we have many familial connections among us: husbands and wives, ex-husbands and ex-wives, girlfriends, boyfriends, sons, cousins, nieces, nephews, bandmates and, of course, old, old friends. I encourage you to find the deep connections you feel in your group and make the play ring with those. I think we did that.

Group Activities:

The Groan Symphony: A group warm-up, filled with body noises and groans, gradually turning into a composed sound piece with discernible themes and variations.

The Vortex: A mandala-like spiral that pulls everyone into it until the group is tightly wound and packed together, then disperses by either literally unwinding, or exploding outward. This can be led by different people, or by the same person each time, but it should be powerful enough to pull everyone into it, so that the whole group winds up and unwinds together.

Ghost Marking: This is the movement of actors going over their lines to themselves, holding their scripts, marking through their blocking and gestures. It is an inward action. This can be happening all the time, or in just one particular moment when everyone except the person speaking is marking out parts.

Ductball: This is a warmup game Curious plays. It is exactly what it sounds like: a ball, made of duct tape, kept aloft by the efforts of the group. The players stand in a circle and bat the ductball around between them. There are no rules other than to keep it in play. It can bounce off things (we call this a hector), it can be tightly controlled, or flying out of control. Try it. It's really fun. The vernacular we used is all made up. Make up your own.

Trip Line: This was the penultimate moment of our show, when everyone except the band lined up at the back of the stage, and, to the pounding rhythm of the refrain, "Today I won't go, today I won't go," (from the song of that title), ran to the front of the stage and tripped, together, just before reaching the lip of the stage. The line then turned around, went quickly back to the first position, and ran again, pell mell, to the front, only to be stopped by this damned tripping. The action is repeated as many times as possible until the end of the song.

Getting Ready

1. Don't you want to get ready?

2. This is me getting ready.

1. You aren't doing anything.

2. I <u>am</u> ready.

1. For what?

2. For this.

1. What is this?

2. This is getting ready.

1. For what, though?

2. I don't know, what are you getting ready for?

1. For when it's time.

2. Time for what?

1. To start…

2. Oh, see, that's the problem. I have started. So I don't have to get ready. I already am ready.

1. You don't seem ready.

2. Well neither do you. Maybe <u>you</u> should get ready.

1. I am getting ready.

2. You aren't doing anything.

1. I'm talking to you about getting ready.

2. That's the way you get ready?

1. Well how do **you** get ready?

2. I am ready, baby.

Memorizing

1. I cannot manage to get that last bit. It just eludes me.

2. You obviously aren't working hard enough.

1. What!! I am working hard. Plenty hard…

2. If you were working hard you would have it.

1. I may not work hard the way you work hard.

2. Obviously not…

1. But I am and do work hard.

2. Ok, how do you do it?

1. How do I work hard?

2. Yeah, how exactly are you going about working? What do you do?

1. Well, I read it over and over…

2. Out loud, or to yourself?

1. Both, first one then the other. Then I say it off the page, holding something over it, you know, for the cues…

2. Ok…

1. Then, I don't know, I just keep doing that, then I ask someone to cue me…

2. At what point does that happen? The asking someone?

1. Well, if you do it too soon, it doesn't work you know, so I usually wait until I have it a bit, some of it…It's awfully irritating to cue someone who hasn't got it at all…

2. Yeah, then what?

1. …Well that's it. By that time, I start to have it.

2. So you let up?

1. Well, I try to keep looking at it, but, you know, life intervenes…

2. There it is. I knew it.

1. What?

2. The old "life intervenes" excuse. Translates into, "I stop working…"

1. It does not.

2. It does. Look, do you start at the beginning and just absolutely not go on until you have it?

1. Well, I take a more global approach… I…

2. No, stop. Just answer the question. Do you start at the beginning and just absolutely not go on until you have it?

1. No, I don't do that.

2. That, if I may say so, is the issue.
You're trying to skip over the hard work.

1. Maybe that is how <u>you</u> work hard, how it works for <u>you</u>, but…

2. No, listen. You struggle, right? There are reasons, sure, but bottom line, you struggle, it isn't happening, you're frustrated, and so is everyone else, I might add, it really inhibits the flow…OK, so question yourself…at the core of it, are you working hard? Are you penetrating the top layer of busyness and activity down to a state of concentration and focus where the words begin to take on a real meaning, a life, inside your body, where you dream them and they change you into something; where your cereal rearranges itself into those words, that language, those dreams, and you see the world through a prism of those ideas and that character's eyes; where, at work, you find the letters you are writing and the phone calls you are making, and the documents you are editing have morphed into more opportunities to explore new facets of this language of being; where you find yourself at home, wondering how you got there, immersed in the tub, mumbling the words over and over, checking back constantly to make sure they are correct; and where your script becomes a tattered cross-referenced indexed underlined annotated behemoth that can't be contained in just a binder but needs a special box to carry it in, something you yourself made out of skin and bones and sinew so it becomes part of your body, growing onto you like an extra brain, a psychic external hard drive of motivations and reasons and understandings that create all the meaning you are ever going to need? Are you working hard, like that?

1. …No, I'm not working that hard…

2. OK, then, that's all I'm saying.

The Place We Are In Right Now 1

(Text from Museum of Contemporary Art staging)

A blackness that emerges out of blackness. The lights switching on to dully shine on a flat black floor, bereft of character, painted over and over, always black. And if a warp occurs, a curling edge, then the trap is set, the black hiding years of gouges except between assaults when tape has been ripped up or a divot has been dug into the soft places by something heavy and sharp and burrowing. And that unsaveable square is unscrewed and taken away, replaced by a perfectly cut fresh piece of floor painted black, flat black, ready for the next gouge.

(Text from Links Hall staging)

A place at the edge of the world doesn't appeal. Who would be there? Who would witness that as a seeing-off-into-the-distance end? How would that be experienced? Would it be on long floors that feel so infinite? So clean and luminous? The world defined by blond wood and planking, the strips varnished within an inch of the their lives and spit shined by sock feet or bare feet leaving infrared trails of intention streaking across them…bending the intention to swoop and shuffle and shuck along. Where the end of the world and the flat stretching span of floor (that is the jumping off point) meet? And politely ask you to take off your shoes?

Creativity *(sung)*

May you be smart enough to want something
May you fill your time with schemes
May you forfeit payoffs accordingly
And may your failures be distinguished by mercy

And then say you took one little thing
And then you turned it into another thing
And then you added a few more things
And then something else happened
You're doing it right

May your theories all be praxis, yeah
May distinctions blow beyond the frame
May your future fictive audience convene
And thumbs you up, oh yeah!

And then say you took one little thing
And then you turned it into another thing
And then you added a few more things
And then something else happened

You're doing it right

There's nothing more than this
It's just a question of what we can see
And what we could see if we could really see

Where's Bryn?

1. Where's Bryn?

2. He's not here?

Stage Manager: 45 minutes...

1. No, 45 was just called... Where the fuck is he?

3. He's probably in the bathroom.

4. No, I just came from there, he isn't in there...

5. Oh no, I bet he got cast...

6. *(As soliloquy)* Cast, to be cast, being cast...Like an ancient process involving being still for many hours, not moving, or subtly shifting just to relieve the pressure, but getting back straightaway to the exact angle and facial expression agreed to, because how else can someone capture the essence of "you" if you cannot be still? So then develops a mystical sense of timing around the hours of patiently waiting for the casting to be complete, waiting because a portrait is being created, a negative form into which will be poured the liquid inspiration that becomes the startling picture of "you," successful "you," "you" in the world, as recognized, as chosen. Being cast means someone saw you, really saw you, affirmed your presence and contended it could be used, put to good use, as material that communicated something to someone, sometime, a "you" that has meaning, and that will be remembered.

7. Wait, he got cast? In what?

5. Maybe he booked that commercial he auditioned for the other day. He was telling me about it...

4. Has anyone asked anyone?

3. I'll ask the stage manager. Maybe she got a call...*(Goes off to do that)*

1. This almost happened one other time. He told me he booked a job the weekend of the show, he would have to miss one night at least… I was freaked out. I got really upset and said that I strongly disagreed with that decision – that's how I put it, "strongly disagreed," what I wanted to say was, "you have got to be fucking kidding me," but I didn't say that.

2. It would be hard to say that to him – he's so nice.

5. Yeah, he's perfect except for this one tiny problem.

7. Well, he wants to make a living.

5. OK, all of us have to make a living, but not when you've agreed to do this work, which you knew wasn't going to pay.

1. He told me that time that he'd warned us it might happen, so we couldn't be pissed off about it. Maybe that was the agreement he thought he was entering into.

5. No, the agreement he was entering into was to do the work, and be in the show. Not do the work and then *not* be in the show.

3. *(Coming back)* Yeah, he just called. He booked a commercial, he won't be here tonight, it's running over.

(Simultaneously)

1. …what…the…fuck. That absolutely…

4. How can he do that?! He'll…

7. This is so fucked up.

5. What's the commercial for? He told me it was a national.

3. He said Mars bars. 3 Musketeers.

2. What?

3. Yeah, it's like something with musketeers, he has to wear tights.

6. (*Soliloquy again*) …A room filled with people who all look exactly like you, dressed like you, aspiring to be cast, like you, and all you have to do is smile, just a simple thing, smile, not even say anything, and it's perfect for you, actually, the best thing because so little is demanded. But, you get in there, it's your turn, and you grimace like a pathetic bitch and you can't raise a smile to save your life, and they look at you like you're nuts, they're waiting, and you try to bring it up, you hike one side of your mouth up, the other side won't budge, it just sits there, so they thank you and usher you out of the room back into the room filled with all the people who look exactly like you, the type you apparently are, and you know <u>they</u> won't have any trouble smiling and performing the simple tasks expected of them, they won't have any trouble being cast…what is wrong with you?

5. Fuckin' A, tights…

4. Why didn't you do an understudy like he said?

1. We don't do understudies…

2. Maybe we should have.

3. Aren't you pissed off? It affects you particularly.

8. Sure, I know it does, and it's really difficult, but I totally understand why he did it. I'd do it if I had the opportunity. You're all just annoyed because you don't have that opportunity.

5. No, we're angry because he's not going to be here. It totally fucks up the show.

Solitary Person: No it doesn't. You can take the first thing, I know that big speech. I can do it.

5. That is so completely weird. But fine, you think you know it?

Solitary Person: No problem.

5.: What, you already memorized it?

Solitary Person: Yes, in fact I did. I kind of thought this might happen. Since he said it might.

5. OK, he said it might, not that it definitely would. *(To #8)* I can't believe you're defending him.

8. I'm not defending him. I'm saying all of us would do it if we were given the opportunity.

5. No way.

8. Yes, you totally would… Turn down great money? That would pay for your life for the next several months? You're telling me that doing this, for free, is more important than making enough money to pay for your life for months? And paying for insurance? So you could then do five projects if you wanted to? With insurance???

5. I would turn it down if it meant missing a performance.

8. You're not being honest with yourself.

5. Hey, you can tell yourself a story about both doing this work *and* having the *things* you want - but it's not possible to do both. You can't have one foot in this world and one foot in the world of things and owning. The worlds don't meet. Not really. Maybe for the last 20 years they seemed to meet, it seemed like you could be middle class and still do this work, but nowhere else in the history of the world did people like us live like that.

8. That's what you tell yourself, in order to explain to yourself why you don't have things, why you're no better off than you used to be. Actually you're worse off. You're more tenuous, less stable. But you covet things. You definitely want things. Being paid makes you an adult. Everyone who is an adult wants to feel like an adult.

5. Maybe that's your idea of being an adult. It isn't mine.

8. When's the last time you went to the dentist?

5. I don't need an iPod or cable TV.

1. Yeah, but you *need* toilet paper, right?

The Place We Are In Right Now 2

(MCA)
The velvety swing of vertical blackness on solid-feeling tuggable runners up so high, the cherry picker is needed to examine them. None of that too familiar pinned together combat cloth left mouldering, hung up again to let gravity pull out decay. Kept, instead, perfectly hung, unwrinkled, in stanzas layered front to back, entrances and exits covered and protected. Waving, undulated mossy pillars of carved space, closing in as far as they can go, till they jerk-stop.

(Links Hall)
It cannot be comforted by any kind of tea. It cannot be soothed. The sound of recurring nightmare rumbling, a blighting, rushing over the time, through the time of speaking, and only pausing, only overspeaking, over-shouting, only a concerted effort to remind oneself that the space is worth it creates marginal acceptance. In the aural glow of triumph over circumstances, you narrate to the sound, "you have not got the better of me, you have not blotted me out or made me weep and quit, you have not asked me my name or what I would like to say, but I will say it, even through your cyclical boorishness… Because your continued gradual appearance, throwing each predictable resistance response into my body, my stance, only makes you weaker and me stronger, because… because I give you permission to drown me out, you motherfucking rumble…" Telling yourself that the secret to being negated is pretending you have chosen negation.

I Need You 1

*(Rehearsing and getting cued...
Not really ready to be cued yet.)*

I guess I do need you,

I think I don't need you,

I wish I didn't need you,

I hope I don't need you,

I don't wish to need you,

I wish to never need you,

I hate needing you,

I need you.

Cunt Addled Sorcery

1. Last night, when you crossed down front, you stepped on my line.

2. It needed stepping on. It was slow in coming.

1. It wasn't slow in coming, it was considered.

2. Considered to be slow in coming. I'd polished the same spoon 4 times.

1. I thought that was working.

2. It wasn't.

1. Says who?

2. Says me. I'm flapping around out there like we have all the time in the world.

1. Haven't we got enough time to say the lines?

2. They are meant to overlap.

1. What? They are not. They're meant to buttress up against each other, maybe, or dovetail, even, but not overlap. You wouldn't hear the speech.

2. Nobody wants to hear the speech anyway. It's terrible, a nightmare, I hate saying it.

1. Well if you hate saying it, you're right, nobody will want to hear it. I think it works.

2. Oh really? In what way does it work?

1. It's a damned good speech, come on, I wish I had it. It's got that great big slamming stuff in the middle, and the long pause thing, and the part that slices through.

2. Take it.

1. Sure right, that'd work well. All I've got is that little thing before that. It's the brevity that kills it. It's barely got time to get going. And when you step on it, forget it, it's over before its begun.

2. Yeah, but it lands. I can hear it landing.

1. It lands if you're doing that thing with your face right before.

2. What thing?

1. The little twitchy thing you do, just before.
It kind of sets the whole thing up for a landing.

2. Oh, I didn't even really know I was doing that. So you need me to….

1. Yeah, that's the key to the whole thing. It's negligible without that.

2. Yeah, but I can't do that unless you're over there.
It doesn't make any sense if I just…

1. That's true. But that one time you were able to be behind me,
and I felt like it was so resonant, you know, like it rang.

2. It only rings if it lands.

1. That's true.

2. OK well, sorry. I'll just wait then. Till you're done.

1. Thanks. I'll pick it up a bit. Try to.

2. Let's run it.

1. OK, OK.

2. You start.

1. From where?

2. …from like, uh…How about from "cunt addled sorcery"…?

1. Oh, uh, wait, no that's weird for me. How about,
from the bit about the cloud?

2. OK, yes, let's see…

It's Not Just You 1

1. Well….

2. Yeah….

1. How's the…

2. Eh.

1. Oh. OK.

2. And did you…

1. No, not yet. I will, I will…It's no big deal, I can wait…

2. Not too long, though.

1. No, I'll go.

2. OK…Were you able to find your…?

1. No, I cannot find it.

2. Shit, that sucks.

1. Yes. It does.

2. Will you have to do all that again?

1. Probably.

2. Ug….You know, I am finding it difficult to do that one part.

1. The fast…?

2. Yes. I just think it's too…

1. Me too.

2. Really? Maybe it's not just me, then.

1. No, no. It's not just you.

2. Whew.

1. Yeah.

Consequences *(sung)*

Can you provide a guarantee
The sun will shine
And we will see
our project grow and grow
Nurture a moment planted so tenderly

We need to get it done

We're needing to get it done
(No matter what the consequences)

In order to build a process huge
One reconciles to subterfuge
In order to build a process deep
One reconciles to lack of sleep

If fate is all it's meant to be
It's somewhat bigger than you or me
And thus we throw our hands up high
We're willing to move both earth and sky

Can you provide a guarantee
That all of us,
Including me
Will see our project grow and grow
Nurture a moment planted so tenderly

We need to get it done

We're needing to get it done
Can we get it done
We'd better get it done
I hope we can get it done
We might not get it done

No matter what the consequences

Something and Nothing

(Either as a soliloquy or as a speech being rehearsed that is also real.)

Nothing is going to save anyone, because something always happens, which for some, is better in the long run, than nothing happening. It's always something or nothing...Now, if Something and Nothing were in the same play, say, they would have to have scenes together right? They would have to be able to stand each other long enough to be in the same space, and that space would have to be able to contain them both, meaning they would have to be willing to share their resources, even meager things like their yoga mats or the mirror, and you gotta know that Something would be more self-effacing than Nothing, Nothing would brood and take up space and be heavily pouting and demanding attention by <u>not</u> demanding attention. Something would be more playful and fluid, more changeable, right? Less monolithic... Or maybe they could find their way into conspiracy, hold their noses and jump off the bridge holding hands, for some higher cause, for the sake of the play...Probably they would have to turn their heads away from each other's breath, not wanting to confront or lash out but wishing the other were a little bit more like them. Maybe the play would be a thinly veiled roman à clef <u>about</u> Something and Nothing, they essentially play themselves, but meta, or they cleverly switch, even back and forth, one night Something the next night Nothing, flipping a coin backstage just the one hour before so that even they felt off base and couldn't plan or prepare too rigidly. But they both have their own takes on it, obviously Something's interpretation of Nothing would be terribly Wuthering Heightsy, kind of romantically nothingish, lots of sighs and impotent rages. Surely, Nothing thinks, watching all that sturm and drang, surely that isn't actually nothing, it's a lot more than nothing, nothing being smaller and more naturalistic, maybe. And Nothing's take on Something might be hilariously overblown, so much of something that it kind of turns into nothing, in which case, Nothing thinks, it's a kind of triumph, because everything is always, at base, kind of nothing...No sincerity in it, Something thinks, watching Nothing portraying Something. And maybe they get to the point where they're kind of sick of trying to portray each other, or subvert each other, and they just give up and stop switching parts, they settle into a rhythm of giving up, which suits Nothing to a T, of course. Something struggles with it but finds a way, as Something is wont to do, to make it work. Hell, even giving up, slipping behind, falling down, laming out can be made into something. So Something thinks. And Nothing thinks nothing, of course...

Unknowing *(sung)*

(A song being rehearsed, badly. Starting over, stopping…One of the people rehearsing the song—should be a woman—gets a phone call mid run-through and has to run off stage.)

I thought I understood the basic workings of the plan as it was outlined to me last year on the phone.

A veritable explosion of ideas and visions crushed into a slapdash soup of mania, a poem…
An explanation of the world.
Nothing less…well, a re-imagining…
A way of looking at the world.
Just think, the grandeur of it all…
A frame that's built around the world.
That's the way it was sold to me.
But really all I've seen, all I've been privy to, the whole of it is something more equivocal, ambivalent, fluxxy, a half formed chopped up freestyle question that betrays the very essence of uncertainty, and in principle, unknown…

The problem is:
I want to know. I 'd rather know. I'd like to know.
I want to know. I 'd rather know. I'd like to know.

Unknowing…It's hard to pay attention to
Unknowing…It creates a lot of tension, this
Unknowing…
I would rather float away…

Childcare

(Cell phone rings, she goes offstage)

1. Oh god now what?

2. The fuckin babysitter? Again?

3. Is everything alright?

2. Oh who knows? It's so fucking hard to work with her right now, she's always unavailable, distracted…

3. Well come on, it's natural…

1. Did you know it was going to last for years, though? I mean, this has been going on for years…

3. Well obviously, yes, I did know. I assumed it.

2. Man, it's so irritating. You just get going and then you have to stop and wait…

3. Come on, it's not her fault.

1. No, it is her fault. Or it's her responsibility. You have to make a choice, this is not compatible with that. This is being away at night. This is not being home for supper. This is not compatible with that.

4. We can work around it…

2. The whole thing hinges on her! We can't work around it…

4. We can. We will.
Don't you think we can extend ourselves that much?

1. OK, yes, of course we can, but still it's difficult having half of a person's attention.

4. Even if we only have half of her attention, that's better attention than you get with most.

2. Yeah, but it brings everything down. I just want to do the work and not deal with external things constantly.

4. That's the price of sticking with it past a certain age.

2. I know, I know.

4. People have families and stuff. It's really pretty normal. Things change.

1. This is too much, though. It just never ends…

2. It all ends. Eventually everyone quits because it's just too hard.

1. That's true. Not too many older folks in the game.

3. So be happy she's still here at all. She could easily say she's just not doing it anymore till the kids are grown. Then, by that time, you're out of the swing and it seems childish and far away, to do anything like this. You tell yourself it's part of your past and it was great, but you've had to grow up and find some stability. Plus it wasn't fun anymore, being exhausted all the time and working on ten things at once and us-against-the-worlding it, you look for the more humble but durable satisfactions. I can totally imagine it, years down the line, being asked to do something, deciding to do it, for old time's sake, but then finding yourself a visitor to it, a tourist, because you left, and it's really hard to come back.

Certainty and Doubt

(Solitary Person says this)

I am very certain that the next thing is always going to happen. There is such certainty in me that no one could ever talk me out of it. Each day, I sit here, and I wait patiently for the next thing, never once for one minute doubting it, but being interested in watching to make sure in any case. I know I'm right. I have the evidence of my experience to back me up, and also I am a person for whom regularity and patterns are very readily noted. Everything is possibly the next thing. This is difficult. Everything is difficult, but this particular difficulty, at least I feel like I have a chance, there's a way to figure it out, to do it differently, to make it all mean something. There can be rules, and I can follow them, and decide to break them, and then change my mind and do it a different way, and the difficulties are different, but it's possible to try again. Because with certainty like this, it's like there is something to focus on, to give my attention to, and then maybe other people will put their attention on it too and then we are sharing that attention, and for a moment at least there might be some kind of consensus or even like a sacerdotal kind of confusion-into-order, something that is reassuring to me about people and the world.

On the other hand, I am also full of doubts about everything. I have a morbid fear that something bad is already secretly happening, either to me, or to someone I love, and the only reason I don't know about it yet is because it's still happening on a cellular level where it couldn't be apprehended even by experts and psychics. I can't really think about what is happening right at the moment, because I feel it is my duty and my avocation to be prepared and thoughtful about what might happen soon or next, or sometime later, so I can be the warning and the voice of attentiveness that others don't seem to have. If anyone tries to tell me that my hair trigger watchfulness is a waste of time, I let them in on my secret: it is possible to ward off the inevitable simply by waving it away at a crucial moment. As disaster strikes, you divert its attention and it may not strike you.

E/e *(sung)*

Indeed we need to feel
Existence being feeling
And the shadowshade visions of our dreams
Indeed we need to feel
Those consequences
Of holding shut the mouth
Ha ha ha ha
It can blow you up

Excruciation
Exuberation
And I wonder
And I wonder how we came to be good friends
Under this backdrop sky
Exasperation
Exaltation
And I wonder
And I wonder if we'll find the many ends
Before we die

We need to feel
That's how you know when something's real
Don't ask me why

Hey! We need to feel
Yeah well, we're all alone
You can use it as a litany
I said we need to feel
Those consequences of holding shut the mouth
Ha ha ha ha
That shit can blow you up....

The Yes Face (sung)

He flips out looking
Turns everything inside out
Driven mad like a Bolshevik radical
Wild eyes whimpering
Things are lost

She slips in not looking
Turns everything off inside
Driven mad like a once free radical
Sad eyes whimpering
Things are lost

They make the do you want to live face
They make the yes face

Things are lost, man
A panoply of things
But still, the looking,
The looking, the looking...
So they disdain checking
Inside the locked out room
Driven made like burnt out radicals
Many eyes whispering
Things are lost

(A big fight among two cast members.
They go off, fighting. Everyone is standing around,
watching, excruciated.)

What It's Like

(This conversation emerges from the excruciated watching of the fight.)

1. You know what this is like? It's like having a paper route and being driven around by your dad with the tailgate down, riding around and jumping off to deliver the paper and then running to jump back on while he drives around, but he's speeding up cause he's that kind of dad, so you have to sprint to catch up and the tailgate is bouncing and you have to leap to get back on and you really think you might not make it….

2. Nah, it's not like that…it's more like being at a treasure hunt and not really being so interested in it because it seems kind of babyish but then the people who are doing it really went all out and made a treasure map on fake parchment and a bunch of swords out of plywood, one for everybody, and you get sucked into the spirit of the thing and start running around like a madman looking for clues, and then when X marks the spot is found, you run over to it and think about starting to dig but everyone else is turning all Lord of the Flies and you get kind of scared, scared enough to climb up on somebody's shoulders and even head if you could in order to get away from the flying sand and crazy manic digging, and when someone shouts out that they hit the treasure chest and the insane digging ramps up even another notch, you know you would climb up onto the highest ground even if it meant pushing another person under in order to stay afloat yourself, and then when they pull the top off of the treasure chest and you see the first glint of gold, whether it's Mardi Gras beads or chocolate Passover gelt, it doesn't really matter, because you find yourself suddenly face down over the edge of the pit scrabbling and shoving everyone's hands out of the way, ready to fight for your share of the booty, even if it is only sand covered golden gumballs…

3. No, it isn't really like that...It's more like...planning to bring your group to a wild place, a place where risks are taken and the safety of all is <u>not</u> assured and the tacit understanding that someone might not make it back is fully clear to everyone, and where the changeability of the day is so unpredictable that no one can hope to rest in a plan and no one can protect themselves from possible catastrophe, and where you will only instruct them to arm themselves with the willingness to be destroyed and rebuilt, the courage to walk directly into the maelstrom, and the eros to fuck the shark, and then when you all arrive at the appointed starting place, ready to march off into the fray just as you really are, as you are in your deepest soul, you realize you picked a place where families and little children come for a Sunday stroll, and your wilderness boots and deet canopies and survival pack camouflage regalia seem like overkill next to their sandals and strollers and instamatics, and you couldn't get lost if you tried...It's more like that...

4. *(This is one of the people fighting, who has come back onstage)*
No, it's not like that...It's more like...It's like proposing a project, something you've never done before, and dressing it up with a lot of language that creates an aura of assurance and confidence, calling it something like, "The Limb: A Performance of Part of a Tree"; and plowing forward with momentum and a kind of barely controlled terror, building out the limb one foot in front of you at a time and willing yourself not to look down, but talking to everyone you know and all of the people who decide things and pay for things about how clear you are about that limb and how strong of a limb it is, what a fantastic unique innovative limb you're building, and how exemplary the documentation of the view from that limb is going to be, and then getting to point where you've built it out as far as it can go, and the date and time of some kind of premiere has arrived, where you have to show the limb, and publicly climb out on it, and you wake up in the middle of the night and realize you haven't got a clue about what you've built and the whole thing is jerry-rigged and rube goldberged and teetering madly and you know damned well it's not going to support shit... It's more like that...

1,2,3. Yeah, you're right, it is kind of like that...

Ductball

Use these terms:

Hector

Help Your Neighbor

Middle

Still in Play

Beans

Bees

Deferment

Donovan

Half-Donovan

Whose Business? Everybody's Business

Horny

1. I can't concentrate.

2. Why not?

1. I'm horny.

2. Ew, I don't want to know that.

1. Well I am. I'm always horny when I'm getting ready, or trying to learn lines, or warming up, or stretching.

2. You get horny when you're learning lines?

1. Yeah, it's like my dick doesn't want my brain to work. I get horny when I'm scared too. Like right before we go on, I could just fuck somebody.

2. Weird…

1. Who knows why? I could say some fanciful thing about eros and how the creative urge is close to the procreative urge and how taking a risk, the risk of failure, is a way to boost your life force and thus your feeling of arousal, and how energy is just that, energy, so any intense energy is going to make you come alive in a different way, and how any negative intense emotion, like fear, wants to be replaced by a more positive intense emotion, like arousal.…I could say all that, but really I think it's just a weird predilection.

2. Do you ever just stop what you're doing and just fuck?

1. No, it's not convenient. It's kind of a private thing…

2. Maybe you should just jerk off…

1. Maybe…

I Need You 2

(Stentorian)

I guess I do need you,

I think I don't need you,

I wish I didn't need you,

I hope I don't need you,

I don't wish to need you,

I wish to never need you,

I hate needing you,

I need you.

Stage Manager: 15 minute call...

Everyone Else: Thank you 15!

It's For Them

1. I just don't feel it.

2. You will, though. Just keep trying. It's there. People can see it.

1. I feel so far away from it. I just can't lift it off the ground.

2. You're overthinking it.

1. No, what's the point without that? Why bother, really?

2. Uh, so maybe other people can have an experience?

1. They aren't, though. They might be watching me acting like I'm having an experience, but I'm not really having one.

2. Well, acting like you're having one is having one. It's the whole point, being able to create the illusion <u>for</u> them. Because they can't do it. Either they haven't got the sensibility, or the capacity… They need you.

1. All I do is go through the motions. I can't stop thinking about bullshit things I have to get done, or something that isn't going well. I feel the flop sweat start to trickle and then I'm done for.

2. They don't know any of that.

1. Who cares about them? I want to have an experience. I want to lift up out of myself and be detached from my body and see myself going through the blocking, saying my lines, and I want to realize with a burst of adrenaline that, it's real, it's really happening…that I'm split in two, my mind floating over my body, watching me do something delicate and indelible.

2. Why don't you climb down off the cloud of unknowing and put your attention on them, consider your presence in front of them a gift, that they don't have to pay attention to you at all, that they are giving that to you, their attention, and so you owe them something, you owe them your attention, to the illusion you are creating, to the insight and articulation you are giving them, because they can't, they can't say it like that, just nail it down hard. Left to their own devices they would wander around and backtrack and leave out important aspects, but you can distill it, cook it down to its essence, put it in your body and in your voice and hand it to them like an intravenous shot of understanding. You can say whatever you want, but really, it's all for them…

1. I want it to be for me.

2. Go watch somebody else do it then. Or do it in private.

The Place We Are In Right Now 3

(MCA)
The wall, the wall, existing in the mind's eye, so vast and overwhelming, demanding attention whenever light shines on it. A place to throw something but what whatever what? The emptiness like an invitation and a taunt: "Whatever could possibly fill this? No imagination could ever be this big…" So what if it is left for shadows to span it, an erotic moan of wasted color and meaning, it's got its legs open, that wall, and is demanding to be artistically fucked.

(Links Hall)
The way the sun comes up in the morning. The way the light flowers in the room on the solstice earliest of earlies, and then dropping out and off, late into summer evenings. Before the fancy light blocker curtains, before the possibility of a black even existed, the only choice was a slow fade, like life, the gradual graying of expectation into a purplish twilight form of darkness, windows open and grasping for air, because the air conditioner came at the time of the curtains, and, sweating, you had to ask yourself: why do we linger and glow towards the waning, and give our power to the slow dawn? Our connections over drumbeats and the exhilarated superiority of the earliest days always felt like a beginning of the end of the beginning… of the end…

Farts

I told you about the last time this happened. You kept talking about cheese and farts and assholes and it just made me sick. I felt like I was going to puke, really, I was, like, cat-gagging the whole time. And even when I asked you guys to stop, you still just armpit farted and raspberried and stuck your butts out at me. It was like I was talking to myself. Nothing ever changes, we just go around and around on an endless wheel of suffering, seeing the same scenes come up again and again on a cyclical basis, old favorites returning, oh yeah, here comes that again, oh, and here is that pain, that hurt, that fear, over and over. And when we try to intercede, to stop the wheel from turning, if we don't just get off the wheel, if we're still on it but try to stop it, then it's just being controlling and willful, and it's all based on stress and inflexibility, and then we have <u>that</u> thing to add to the wheel, which will just come around again and we'll be forced to revisit <u>that</u> experience.

So can you please just stop talking about farts???

I'm Here (sung)

(Sung by the Solitary Person at first. Everyone else joins eventually.)

I'll stand here alone
Or I'll stand here with you
But I'm going to stand here, yeah...

I'll stand here in black
Or I'll stand here in blue,
But I'm going to stand here, yeah...

All that basement coming back at me...
I've got a case of 8 o'clock in the mornings...
But I know I can't give in...

So I'll stand here alone
Or I'll stand here with you
But I'm going to stand here, yeah...

I'll stand here all broke
Or I'll stand here with glue,
But I'm going to stand here, yeah...

Too much nuh-uh as far as I can see...
I've had my fill of broken bulbs on the stairway
And I know I can't give in...

I'll stand here alone
Or I'll stand here with you
But I'm going to stand here, yeah...

I'll stand here with lies
Or I'll stand here true,
But I'm going to stand here, yeah...

I Need You 3

(To audience)

I guess I do need you,

I think I don't need you,

I wish I didn't need you,

I hope I don't need you,

I don't wish to need you,

I wish to never need you,

I hate needing you,

I need you.

Stage Manager: 5 minute call...

Everyone: Thank you, five!

Fiefdom

1. I am not doing this anymore. After this—that's it, no more.

2. You always say that.

1. Yeah, but this time I mean it. I am over this shit, I cannot take it anymore. I just don't enjoy it, the same old fucking thing over and over, I'm always thinking it's going to be good this time, we are going to do something different this time, we won't fight, we'll find new things. But it's always the same, every day. I feel like I'm wearing a scratched up pair of old glasses, can't see a thing through them, all I would have to do is change them or take them off, but I just never do.

2. That's not our fault. You always act like your bad mood or bad experiences are our fault. It's you who are the big bummer.

1. Then why ask me to do it? Why ask me to be here?

2. Because you're good, obviously, it's always better when you're in it, you bring the joy, even if you are a moody pill and a dick.

1. I wouldn't be as moody if we didn't have to reinvent the wheel every single time.

2. What's that supposed to mean?

1. It means nothing ever grows or gets better. I feel like I come in here ready to take it to the next level, but we just stay stuck on the same old boring level.

2. Levels…That's video game-speak. I don't live in that world.

1. You don't live in any world. You just live in your own little fiefdom.

2. Fiefdom? I don't have a fiefdom.

1. Yes you do. All of this.
It's all yours, you made it so you think you own it.

2. OK yes, I did make it. I did. Through years of hard work.
So why wouldn't I care about how it's made?
I care the most, so I work the hardest. So fine…

1. Yes fine, sure, but you don't work the hardest…

2. What is that supposed to mean?

1. Just what I said. You act like you're working hard, but you coast, you don't do the work to make it better, you're contented just to keep it the same. You want me here to serve you. If I have an independent thought or express an opinion, you roll right over it.

2. Not if it's interesting.

1. Interesting to whom? I find my thoughts quite interesting.

2. Then you can go off and make your own thing. I'm so sick of people. Treating me like…

(Improvise here depending on specific circumstances of the performing company)

…And yet you reserve the right to complain…Maybe I don't do it to your satisfaction, but at least I do it.

1. That's right, you don't do it to my satisfaction.

2. Fine, then run away and hide, don't stand up to it and measure yourself against it.

1. I can't measure myself against it! I could never do what you do. I'm not claiming I could. I think I can be <u>better</u>. I'm only saying I think it can be better.

Today I Won't Go (sung)

Today I won't go today I won't go today I won't go today I won't go
Today I won't go today I won't go today I won't go today I won't go

As I get older I am always overpacking
So worried there might be some kinda situation
I just don't want to face another charming faux pas
If only I can have the proper accoutrement handy for where I'm going

As I get older I am always sick when I travel
For some odd reason motion makes me feel uneasy
There's nothing for it but to sit and wish for the end
If I could just wake up and already be wherever I was going…

Take me take me take me I'll go…

As I get older I am always leaving something
I fool myself by thinking I can keep that back door open
But if I check then I will surely notice
I don't have the key to where it is I think that I am going…
So…

Today I won't go today I won't go today I won't go today I won't go
Today I won't go today I won't go today I won't go today I won't go

Trip Line

(As described in introductory note.)

Stage Manager: Places, please.

End of the show: Melee to get into places. Getting organized.

Last image: line of performers across the stage, everyone looking at the audience with an expectant body, ready to begin.

Blackout.

– The End –

EPILOGUE:

AN OUTRO-DUCTION

A maker, who writes & composes; a performer, who sings and speaks with unmistakably insightful voices, stances and demeanors—be they her own songs and shows or those of Beckett or Brecht, of her brother, Bryn Magnus, or of her creative partner, Beau O'Reilly; a teacher and outside-eye, who will give young work the very attention young work needs, so scarce in hurried, hackneyed and overwhelmed times; a musician who composes within recording studios.

> *"Who? Jenny Magnus? Do you know Jenny Magnus? Huh! I know Jenny Magnus… Are YOU Jenny Magnus?"*

This bit of repartée, this in-joke, has been mumbled between us for much of the twenty-some years our conversation has been going on. It is our wry receipt of the place, which an avant-garde, fringe, visionary or experimental maker and performer occupies in public life. If you are as surprising, and surprisingly familiar, as Jenny, everyone has heard of you and no one knows who you are.

Jenny taught me to consider 'Introspectacle.' I met her in a politically charged time, in which the failures and follies of the world distracted me from my own affairs. Jenny surprised me when she insisted upon encountering this world while remaining present, culpable and implicated, square in herself. No ideal, however sweet, distracts entirely from the plain and profane bodily slog of truth.

By keeping such, and other, conflicts alive—rather than according them resolves and redemptions like pop culture demands but which are false to any body of truth: Jenny Magnus is a body of truth. Her sense of humor comes from within, from the thick of it, rather than from distance. In Berlin, when her solo show was invited to a venue there, she pulled audience chairs closer and tighter around her in rehearsal; the house managers solicitously replaced them at their traditional distance and, upon returning before her show, she moved them in close again. Sometimes her explosive torso almost lunges out over the front row, other times her quiet pondering seems almost private: we are invited to share a room in which quite immediate presence is radical and live.

– **Stefan Brün** / Chicago, IL / 2013

Observations of an Orchestrated Catastrophe:

ARTIST PROFILE

Jenny Magnus is an interdisciplinary artist who brings composition, intention, rhythm, dynamics and inventiveness to every form of art-making she encounters. She has created hybrid integrations of performance, music, theatrical imagery and philosophy in her explorations and meditations about awareness, attention, and the "performative moment." Her performances ride a shifting line between singing and speaking, talking about thinking while thinking about talking, and incoporating live with mediated images.

She is a founding co-Artistic Director of the Curious Theatre Branch. She has also shown work at Steppenwolf Theater, at the Museum of Contemporary Art in Chicago, at the former Lunar Cabaret, at the Prop Thtr, and on tours throughout America and Europe.

She was a longtime member of the band Maestro Subgum and the Whole, and now records with the Crooked Mouth. Her intrepid curiousity about being present in front of people has also led to an active teaching career in which she brings a conscious intention to challenge students of all ages, in varied situations, to see themselves as the authors of their own education striving for excellence in their attention and intention. For more information see: **jennymagnus.com**

www.ingramcontent.com/pod-product-compliance
Lightning Source LLC
Chambersburg PA
CBHW020901080526
44589CB00011B/391